PENGUIN BOOKS

EASY COOKING IN RETIREME

After a career covering nutrition research, broadcasting, writing and lecturing, Louise Davies has now retired. But she remains actively involved as a Consultant in Gerontology Nutrition and as Honorary Senior Lecturer at the Royal Free Hospital School of Medicine in London.

Dr Davies is an adviser to Euronut-Seneca (a concerted action project on nutrition and health of the elderly in the European Community). As Vice Chairman of the Committee on Nutrition and Ageing of the International Union of Nutritional Sciences, she is currently engaged in cross-cultural studies on food habits and health in later life. She is a Fellow of the Institute of Home Economics, an Accredited Nutritionist and an honorary associate of the British Dietetic Association.

She is the author of *Easy Cooking for One or Two*, which was published by Penguin in 1972 (2nd revised edition 1988), *Easy Cooking for Three or More* (1975) and *More Easy Cooking for One or Two* (1979).

Louise Davies

Easy Cooking in Retirement

PENGUIN BOOKS

PENGUIN BOOKS

Published by the Penguin Group
Penguin Books Ltd, 27 Wrights Lane, London w8 5tz, England
Penguin Books USA Inc., 375 Hudson Street, New York, New York 10014, USA
Penguin Books Australia Ltd, Ringwood, Victoria, Australia
Penguin Books Canada Ltd, 10 Alcorn Avenue, Toronto, Ontario, Canada m4v 3b2
Penguin Books (NZ) Ltd, 182–190 Wairau Road, Auckland 10, New Zealand

Penguin Books Ltd, Registered Offices: Harmondsworth, Middlesex, England

First published 1993

10 9 8 7 6 5 4 3 2 1

Filmset in 12/14 pt Monophoto Baskerville
Typeset by Datix International Limited, Bungay, Suffolk
Printed in England by Clays Ltd, St Ives plc

Contents

Acknowledgements

My grateful thanks to all the friends — retired and not yet retired — who have generously given me their favourite recipes.

In addition, a special acknowledgement to British Gas for a 'cook-in' to test new recipes and cookery methods; and for advice from colleagues at the Electricity Council, Food from Britain Information Service, Kellogg Company of GB, Milk Marketing Board, National Dairy Council, Butter Council, Van den Berghs, and the information services of British Meat, Trout, Chicken, Turkey and Poussin, Scottish Salmon and Farmhouse English Cheese.

Gill Balen, Dorothy Lawson and Evelyn Currie shared with me manuscript copies of recipes collected over the years; Barbara Simpson of Le Faux Pas, Southgate, and Penny Beral (Catering) suggested recipes for the 'Entertaining' chapter; Frankie Raiher and Barbara Frais introduced me to the microwave; and Sue Thomas advised on 'Maximum Nourishment' as well as 'Cooking for Children'.

A special thank you to my daughters: Paula, who

suggested many original recipes for this book and helped
to amend the first draft, and Ruth who advised on food
technology. Both joined in the tasting (and clearing
up) sessions with Richard, Tony, Frank, Helen and
Kathleen.

A Note on Quantities

In some of the recipes liquids are measured in cups or wine glasses; any variation in size would not matter unduly in these cases, but an average British teacup holds 6–7 fl oz (170–200 ml) and a wine glass holds approximately 3½ fl oz (100 ml). The standard teaspoon holds 5 ml, the tablespoon 15 ml; when measuring solids, *level* spoonfuls should be used.

Egg Sizes

0 = 75 g plus
1 = 70–75 g
2 = 65–70 g
3 = 60–65 g
4 = 55–60 g
5 = 50–55 g

These are the weights on the day of packing; the eggs will lose weight through evaporation with keeping. Packers may include a larger egg in the pack if they need to make up weight. Unless stated otherwise, the recipes in this book use size 3 eggs.

Chapter One
A Note on Quantities

Chapter One
Maximum Nourishment

This chapter could be summed up in a single word: MODERATION. If you already EAT SOMETHING OF EVERYTHING AND NOT TOO MUCH OF ANY ONE THING, thus including a wide variety of foods, you are well on the path to maximum nourishment.

However, retirement often brings a change in lifestyle that can affect meal patterns and nutritional choice: there may be changes in meal companions, meal times, housing, shopping, income, activity, loneliness or happiness ... You may, or may not, make more time for leisurely breakfasts or eating out. The nutritional decisions you make now could help to prevent a downward spiral in health as you grow older. But be careful: those decisions could be for the better or for the worse. Nowadays we are constantly being bombarded with dietary advice, most of it contradictory, much of it confusing and some of it downright sensational and misleading.

Some time ago, a national newspaper made a list of foods that have been both recommended as 'good for you' *and* blamed as 'bad for you', depending on which self-appointed guru was pronouncing. They included: decaffeinated coffee, butter, red meat, crisps, milk, potatoes, peanuts, apples, bread, chocolate and eggs; and fish said to be so full of mercury that one wit suggested you should take your temperature with an anchovy!

A dietitian friend of mine puts all this in perspective with the following analogy: if you hit your arm hard, it will bruise; but if you give it a series of moderate taps, you will have no damage. In other words, unless you have specific health problems with them, there are no bad foods, if you eat them in moderation.

The following paragraphs should help you to find a way through the maze of conflicting advice. They cover the questions most frequently put to me in my lectures to men and women before and after the age of retirement from work.

The recipes in this book are designed to endorse this advice so that you can enjoy eating for better health.

Osteoporosis and calcium

For each individual there are pros and cons for hormone replacement therapy – that is a subject for medical counselling.

Calcium supplements alone have not been shown to be effective in preventing significant bone loss (osteoporosis). However, it is prudent, and particularly important around the menopause, to keep up the intake of calcium foods to replace the calcium that is constantly being lost from the bones. Best food sources: milk (this includes skimmed or semi-skimmed as well as full-cream milk), cheese, yogurt and similar dairy foods, fish that are eaten with their bones (e.g. sardines), vegetables and nuts. For bone strength it is better to drink hard water than hard alcohol!

One of the best preventive measures against osteoporosis: keep active.

Activity

For bone strength you need load-bearing exercise: better where possible to walk up the stairs than take the lift.

Walk every day (for at least twenty minutes) as briskly as possible. Or, if you prefer, do gardening, DIY, dancing or other sports (swimming is a good muscle-toning exercise but not so effective for the prevention of osteoporosis when floating takes the load off the bones).

If you find walking difficult, try the prop of pushing your grandchild in a pushchair (if you don't have a grandchild, borrow someone else's – with permission!).

Sitting in a rocking chair is better than lying down on a bed or sofa to rest. If chairbound seek suitable exercises.

Activity comes under the heading of nutritional advice, because increasing activity (energy expenditure) allows you to eat nourishing foods (energy intake) without putting on more weight. This minimizes the risk of marginal nutritional deficiencies.

Sunlight and vitamin D

Vitamin D is also needed for bone strength.

Best food sources: fatty fish, and foods fortified with vitamin D, such as breakfast cereals, margarine and some processed milks.

Main source: the action of sunlight on the skin. In this country, the rays of the sun are most effective for vitamin D production between the months of May and October and between the times of 11 a.m. and 4 p.m. (best around midday).

In retirement, during these periods, avoid overpowering sunshine but try to get into the sunlight, even on a cloudy day, for about one or two hours each day (push back sleeves, open up collars). If confined to the house let a shaft of sunlight fall on the hand or other exposed skin through an *open* window (glass cuts off beneficial rays). If you can, take advantage of cut-price winter holidays in the sun. Obviously, with current concerns about risks of skin cancer versus risks of osteoporosis, the message is again one of moderation: don't overdo the sunbathing but enjoy sufficient sunlight.

Arthritis

Many diets have been recommended for the alleviation of arthritis. Some seem to give relief from pain to some patients, so they are worth trying, under supervision. Unfortunately so far no diet has been found to be effective for all sufferers.

Dietary fibre

Increasing dietary fibre can markedly relieve constipation and is recommended, particularly as one gets older, for the prevention of diverticulosis.

The normal diet, including foods such as bread, potatoes, cereals, vegetables and fruit should provide plenty of roughage (now referred to with more scientific accuracy as 'dietary fibre' or 'non-starch polysaccharides'). If you enjoy them, choose wholemeal and wholegrain breads and cereals, and include pulses (peas, beans and lentils) and other high fibre foods, which are now readily available. But when adding any new fibre foods to your diet, go easy: too much can give you an internal hurricane!

'Doses' of natural bran or laxatives may make minerals such as calcium, zinc and iron unavailable to the body. Try instead food partnerships which add these minerals along with the fibre, e.g. high-fibre breakfast cereals with milk, sweetened with raisins or sultanas.

Fluids

We need at least eight cups of non-alcoholic fluid a day for optimum health. Make sure you drink this even if you don't feel thirsty (alcohol – although it may have other advantages – increases dehydration, and that can cause headaches and confusional states). Plenty of drinks are especially important for those on a high-fibre diet.

To avoid getting up in the night, drink earlier in the day – not just before bedtime. If taking diuretics or water pills you still need just as many drinks.

Dietary iron

A diet rich in iron can help to prevent anaemia, with the tiredness and general malaise that it brings. The best sources of iron include meat, offal and eggs. Other good sources: vegetables, pulses, wholemeal bread and breakfast cereals, but these need vitamin C to help the absorption of iron; particularly good are combinations of the two, such as citrus juice for breakfast with cereals.

Overweight

If you feel overweight, is it because of current fashions? In spite of the ever-optimistic headlines, 'crash diets' are almost certainly doomed to failure: for long-term weight control you need an eating pattern that can happily be continued for months and years. Mild overweight is not generally a health hazard, and if your metabolism has slowed down, the effort of dieting may not be worth the results obtained. Excessive underweight may be more of a health risk.

You may be medically advised to lose weight if it is interfering with your mobility or you need surgery; or if your weight is exacerbating conditions such as diabetes, arthritis, high blood pressure or coronary heart disease.

Do not cut out meals: eat frequent, but *small* meals (try the dodge of using smaller plates); cut down high-fat items, also high-sugar foods and alcohol. Dietary fat reduction is *not* generally advised for the 'old old'.

Fats and cholesterol

Cholesterol is a normal constituent of body tissues, with many valuable functions. But too much can narrow the blood vessels and damage the heart. Your doctor will counsel you, via a dietitian and nurse, if it is thought that you need to reduce cholesterol levels with diet and weight control. But don't panic! A stressful lifestyle raises cholesterol levels.

Reducing your intake of saturated (animal) fats will help to lower a raised blood cholesterol: eat less of the high-fat dairy foods (switch to skimmed or semi-skimmed milk, low-fat cheeses, low-fat yogurts and fromage frais); cut visible fat off meat; eat more fruit and vegetables.

Polyunsaturated fats, fish oils and virgin olive oil have all been recommended for prevention of coronary heart disease. Again, moderation is the key: do not over-indulge in any of them. A pleasant way of reducing total fat consumption is to switch to 'dry frying' in the new-style pans, and use alternative methods of fat-free cooking such as the microwave, steamer or grill.

Health foods and nutritional supplements

The term 'health foods' is misleading: *all* foods can contribute to a healthy balanced diet. 'Natural' does not always mean 'safe'. Some supplements sold in health food shops provide nutrients far in excess of recommendations: some nutrients are harmless in excess, but others are potentially toxic. If you feel you need supplements without having been advised to take them by a doctor, first ask yourself what is wrong with your food choice and meal patterns?

I hope that the recipes in this book will prove more tempting to you than pills and potions.

Chapter Two
Minimum Effort

SOUPS

Parsnip, carrot and orange soup
Vegetable soup with barley

VEGETABLES

Cabbage and capers
Carrot and courgette fritters
Carrots and celeriac (buttered)
Cauliflower, leeks and greens
Chinese leaves (fried)
Courgette medley (microwave)
Vegetables in sauce
    carrots in white sauce
    broad beans in parsley sauce
    leeks in cheese sauce
    broccoli florets in egg sauce
    Jerusalem artichokes in tomato sauce
    beetroot, or shredded cos lettuce, in lemon sauce
    runner beans in chunky onion sauce
Kale and lemon

Honeyed potatoes
Lyonnaise potatoes (microwave)

SAUCES

Cranberry and marmalade
Watercress

SALADS

Cheese, fruit and nut salads
Vinaigrette dressings
Orange and carrot salad

SNACKS

Devilled toasted cheese
Fresh pasta with cheese sauce
Puff-pastry tarts
    tomato, cheese and mustard tart
    mushroom and onion tart
Spaghetti bolognese (vegetarian)
Stuffed courgette (or pepper) bake
Vegetable crumble

FISH

Baked stuffed fillets of fish
Grilled fish fillet with cheese-crumb topping
Pan-fried plaice with orange sauce
Scottish salmon (grilled)
Tuna avocado bake

POULTRY

Chicken with apricot sauce
Crisp spiced chicken
Herbed chicken (low fat)

MEAT

Gammon steak with apple and spiced cider
Beef and mushrooms in sour cream
Pork chops in rosemary, orange and pepper sauce
Lamb chops with peach chutney
Stir fry
Veal escalope (low fat)

DESSERTS

Avocado with pink grapefruit juice
Crunchy apple and nut creams
Hot orange dessert
Minted melon with raspberries or orange
Pears in red wine
Summer fruit crumble
Yorkshire rhubarb crisp

SUMMER BEVERAGE

Instant iced coffee shake

Parsnip, carrot and orange soup

Serves 2–3

INGREDIENTS

8 oz (225 g) parsnips (about 3 small)
4 oz (115 g) carrots (about 1 large)
2 oz (55 g) onion (about ½ medium)
1 tablespoon oil
small knob margarine or butter
1 vegetable stock cube
⅛ teaspoon ground ginger
⅛ teaspoon sugar
a few grinds of pepper
1 sliver orange zest (outer peel without pith)
juice of ½ orange

METHOD

1 Slice the peeled vegetables and fry them gently in the oil
  and butter for 10 minutes to soften without browning.
2 Make up the vegetable stock to ¾ pint (425 ml) with
  boiling water and add to the pan with the ginger,
  sugar, pepper and orange zest.
3 Simmer with the lid on the pan until the vegetables
  are tender, approximately 25–30 minutes.
4 Sieve or liquidize. Can be frozen at this stage.
5 Return to the pan to reheat with the orange juice
  just before serving.

Vegetable soup with barley

Serves 4 (quantities can be halved for 2 portions, or some can be frozen for later use)

INGREDIENTS

4 oz (115 g) each carrots, celery, swede, parsnip
1 medium onion
1 oz (30 g) butter or margarine
1 clove garlic, crushed
2 pints (1.1 litre) chicken stock
1–2 tablespoons tomato purée
1 bay leaf
2 oz (55 g) pearl barley
salt and pepper
croûtons to serve

METHOD

1 Cut the peeled and trimmed vegetables into dice, making them as even in size as possible. *Alternatively*, grate coarsely in a food processor.
2 Heat the butter or margarine in a saucepan, add the vegetables and garlic, and fry gently until just golden.
3 Pour in the stock with the tomato purée, bay leaf and barley.
4 Bring slowly to the boil and season, then cover and simmer for about 20–30 minutes. The vegetables should be tender and the barley soft.
5 Adjust seasoning and serve with croûtons.

Cabbage and capers

Serves 2

INGREDIENTS

½ lb (225 g) cabbage (firm white or Primo)
a knob of butter
salt and pepper
1 dozen capers, or more to taste
5 fl oz (140 ml) carton soured cream

METHOD

1 Shred the washed cabbage fairly finely.
2 Fry gently in a little melted butter, stirring it around
  to coat it with the fat. Season lightly, put a lid on the
  pan so that the cabbage steams and begins to soften
  in its own juice for a few minutes. Shake the pan
  occasionally to prevent burning or sticking.
3 Stir in the capers and the soured cream, and heat
  gently to warm through.

Note: to avoid curdling use only a little butter and do
not boil the cream.

Carrot and courgette fritters

Serves 2–3

INGREDIENTS

½–1 cup carrots, finely grated*
½–1 cup courgettes, finely grated*
1 shallot or half small onion, finely chopped
1 egg, beaten
2 level tablespoons self-raising flour
½ level teaspoon salt
pinch of pepper
sunflower or corn oil for frying

METHOD

1 Place the grated vegetables in a sieve or colander for 10 minutes to allow moisture, if any, to drain away.
2 In a bowl mix together all the ingredients except the oil.
3 Using a heavy frying-pan, heat less than ¼ inch (½ cm) oil. When it is hot, lift in tablespoonfuls of the mixture, flattening each with a fork.
4 Fry over moderate heat for about 4 minutes on each side to cook and brown.
5 Drain on kitchen paper and serve hot.

* When buying, allow approximately 1 large or two small courgettes and the same amount of carrots.

Carrots and celeriac (buttered)

Serves 2

INGREDIENTS

4 oz (115 g) carrots, peeled
4 oz (115 g) celeriac, peeled
approximately 2 oz (55 g) butter
salt, pepper and nutmeg

METHOD

1 Grate the vegetables together, choosing a coarse rather than a fine grater.
2 Liberally butter a circle of greaseproof paper cut to fit closely into the top of a thick saucepan.
3 Melt the rest of the butter in the pan, add the grated vegetables and season. Press on the buttered greaseproof paper to cover.
4 Put the lid on the pan and cook over a very low heat for about 15–20 minutes. The vegetables should cook gently in their own steam without browning.
5 Taste for seasoning. If you wish, stir in a little more butter before serving.

Cauliflow

eens

Serves 2

INGREDIENTS

3 oz (85 g) cauliflower florets
3 oz (85 g) leeks
3 oz (85 g) spring greens
2 tablespoons margarine
1 teaspoon sugar
salt and white pepper

METHOD

1 Wash and trim the vegetables. Cut the cauliflower into small, even-sized florets. Cut the leeks and greens across in ½–1 inch (1–2 cm) strips.
2 Heat ¼ pint (140 ml) water with the margarine, sugar and seasoning in a saucepan and when the fat has melted, add all the vegetables. Place the lid tightly on the pan.
3 Simmer gently until just cooked, approximately 7–10 minutes. Serve with the cooking liquor.

...ves (fried)

Chi... are generally served raw in a crisp salad
(see ...een Salad, page 291), but they can equally
well be ...ed crisp and hot.

Serv... 2

INGREDIENTS

½ small head Chinese leaves
1 tablespoon oil
juice of 1 lime or ½ lemon

METHOD

1 Shred the Chinese leaves fairly finely.
2 Fry in hot oil for a few minutes, stirring constantly to
   distribute the heat evenly.
3 Lift out with a slotted spoon to drain from the oil
   and sprinkle generously with lime or lemon juice.

Courgette medley (microwave)

This dish uses very little fat and no salt. It can be re-heated in the microwave to serve again next day.

Serves 4

INGREDIENTS

2 medium courgettes, sliced into rounds
1 medium onion, finely sliced and separated into rings
1 teaspoon dried basil
2 medium tomatoes, sliced
½ red pepper, seeded and sliced
2 tablespoons oil (olive or salad)
½ cup grated Parmesan cheese *or* Cheddar cheese, *or* a mixture of breadcrumbs, dried herbs and grated cheese

METHOD

1 Arrange the courgettes in a 1½ quart (1¾ litre) round or oval microwave casserole.
2 Place the onion rings over the top and sprinkle with the basil.
3 Arrange the tomatoes and red pepper over the onion. Pour the oil over the top.
4 Cover and cook on High (600–700 watts) for 5–6 minutes.
5 Sprinkle with cheese or breadcrumb mixture. Cook uncovered for an additional 1–2 minutes to melt the cheese. Serve immediately.

Vegetables in sauce

Freshly cooked vegetables go further and add variety to the meal when they are stirred into a well-flavoured white sauce. The following combinations of vegetables and sauce are among my favourites:

carrots in white sauce
broad beans in parsley sauce
leeks in cheese sauce
broccoli florets in egg sauce
Jerusalem artichokes in tomato sauce
beetroot, or shredded cos lettuce, in lemon sauce
runner beans in chunky onion sauce.

Speedy all-in-one white sauce

Serves 2

INGREDIENTS

1 oz (30 g) butter or margarine, cut up small
1 oz (30 g) flour
½ pint (285 ml) milk (semi-skimmed or full cream)
salt, pepper and nutmeg

METHOD (for all but onion sauce)

1 Put the flour and cut-up fat in the milk in a saucepan and leave for 1 minute for the flour to soften.
2 Bring slowly to the boil, whisking constantly (best with a balloon whisk), and simmer gently for 2–3 minutes until thickened. Season to taste.

3 Now add one of the following:

For parsley sauce
1–2 tablespoons finely chopped or snipped parsley

For cheese sauce
2 heaped tablespoons grated medium-matured
    Cheddar cheese
½ teaspoon mustard

For egg sauce
1 chopped hard-boiled egg

For tomato sauce
equal quantities tomato ketchup and tomato purée,
first stirring in a teaspoon of each and then tasting
for flavour and adding more if desired

For lemon sauce
2–3 teaspoons lemon juice
½–1 teaspoon sugar, to taste

METHOD (for onion sauce)

1 Sweat 1 chopped onion in ½ oz (15 g) butter or
margarine until softened but not brown.
2 Add another ½ oz (15 g) butter or margarine, stir in
1 oz (30 g) flour and cook for a minute or two.
Gradually add ½ pint (285 ml) milk, stirring until
smooth. Season and cook for 2 or 3 minutes.

Hint: to save washing up, first steam or boil the vegetables (except for lettuce or cooked beetroot). Drain and
put to one side in a covered bowl. Use the pan to make
the sauce. Stir in the vegetables to reheat.

Kale and lemon

Look for kale or curly kale, a strong-flavoured green vegetable, at the greengrocers round about Hallowe'en: it is usually in the shops at the end of October or the beginning of November. The lemon in this recipe makes it tasty, and also more nutritious because the iron in the vegetable is more easily absorbed in combination with the vitamin C in the lemon.

Serves 2

INGREDIENTS

1 lb (450 g) curly kale
juice of 1 lemon

METHOD

1 Wash the kale thoroughly and tear into pieces, discarding the thick stems.
2 Put an inch or so (2.5 cm) of lightly salted water in the saucepan and, with the lid tightly on, boil the kale for about 5 minutes until just tender.
3 Drain and sprinkle with the lemon juice before serving.

Honeyed potatoes

Serves 2–3

Oven temperature: 190°C, 375°F, gas mark 5

Cooking time: approximately 40 minutes

You will need a small roasting tin.

INGREDIENTS

1 lb (450 g) new salad potatoes
2 oz (55 g) butter or block margarine
½–1 tablespoon cooking oil
salt
1 tablespoon clear honey

METHOD

1 Scrub or scrape the potatoes. Put into boiling water, bring back to the boil and simmer for 2–3 minutes. Drain.
2 In the preheated oven, melt the butter or margarine and oil, stir in the potatoes, sprinkle with a little salt and roast, basting occasionally.
3 In the last 15 minutes add a tablespoon of clear honey and baste once or twice until well coated and golden.

Lyonnaise potatoes (microwave)

The small amount of oil ensures a crisp texture.

Serves 2

INGREDIENTS

2 medium potatoes, peeled
garlic salt
garlic powder
paprika
1 small–medium onion, finely chopped
2 tablespoons oil
parsley

METHOD

1 Slice the potatoes thinly and evenly. Pat dry with kitchen paper.
2 Arrange a thick layer of potatoes in a microwave dish just large enough to accommodate all the potatoes being used.
3 Sprinkle lightly with the garlic salt, garlic powder and paprika, and top with a layer of chopped onion. Repeat this layering, finishing with a potato layer. Pour the oil over the top.
4 Cover and cook on High (600–700 watts) until the potatoes are tender when prodded with a fork (about 10 minutes, but test after 7–8 minutes).
5 Sprinkle with parsley before serving.

Cranberry and marmalade sauce

Savoury: serve warm with poultry.
Sweet: serve cold with mashed bananas and sour cream.

INGREDIENTS

½ teacup sugar
6 oz (170 g) fresh or frozen cranberries
1 tablespoon of a full-flavoured Seville orange marmalade,
   home-made (page 220) or a tangy, shop-bought variety

METHOD

1 Stir ½ teacup water and the sugar over medium heat
   to dissolve, and then bring to the boil.
2 Add the cranberries, bring back to the boil, simmer
   gently until tender (approximately 10 minutes), with
   occasional stirring. They will 'pop' as they cook, so
   put the lid over the pan to avoid splashes.
3 Stir in the marmalade and taste for flavour.

Watercress sauce

A fresh, bright green, fatless sauce to serve with meats or fish.

You will need a blender or processor to purée the sauce.

Serves 2–3

INGREDIENTS

1 shallot or ½ small onion, peeled and chopped
¼ pint (140 ml) stock
1 bunch watercress
1 level tablespoon flour
pinch of nutmeg
salt and pepper

METHOD

1 Soften the onion in 3 or 4 tablespoons of the stock.
2 Add the chopped watercress and stir over medium heat until it softens (about 3 minutes).
3 Stir in the flour, nutmeg, salt and pepper, add the rest of the stock and bring to the boil.
4 Purée and taste for seasoning.
5 Reheat the sauce before serving.

Cheese, fruit and nut salads

Ring the changes for lunch with a nourishing, attractive mixture of salad vegetables, cheeses, fruits and nuts. When catering for small numbers, use packs of ready-prepared mixed salad vegetables to add variety without waste.

The permutations and combinations ensure variety without boredom. Here are a few suggestions:

Stilton cheese, ripe pear, pecan nuts with vinaigrette dressing (including nut oil) on a bed of green leaves and radicchio.

Bel Paese, banana, raw peanut kernels, mixed endive salad, including escarole, frisée and radicchio.

Walnut cheese (or cream cheese, and pine nuts which have been gently fried without fat to brown), with raspberries and firm salad greens (try lamb's lettuce); vinaigrette with 1–2 teaspoons raspberry vinegar.

Curd cheese (stiffened with crushed digestive biscuits, rolled into small balls and coated with crushed dried walnuts), with melon balls, seedless black grapes or pieces of red plum, on a bed of shredded salad leaves e.g. Lollo Rosso.

Cottage cheese, fresh dates, orange segments, watercress, hazelnuts. If a dressing is needed for the watercress, try a vinaigrette including some hazelnut oil.

(*Continued overleaf.*)

Red Leicester, Cox's apple (quartered, cored, sliced but unpeeled), grated celeriac in lightly curried mayonnaise, on a bed of Lollo Rosso.

Feta cheese, pistachio nuts, avocado, tomato, black olives, chopped herbs, vinaigrette.

Parmesan cheese (thinly sliced with a potato peeler), mango or nectarine, pickled herring, unroasted peanuts, radicchio and endive; dill to garnish.

Gouda cheese, sliced pear, kiwi fruit, apple (unpeeled), pecan nuts or dried walnuts, on a bed of shredded Iceberg lettuce or Chinese leaves. Sprinkle the fruit with lemon juice. Can be served with a dressing of yogurt, mayonnaise and crumbled blue cheese (or a ready-bought Blue Cheese Dressing).

Vinaigrette dressings

Oil and vinegar dressings are usually 1 part vinegar to 2–3 parts oil, plus sugar, salt, pepper, mustard, and other flavourings to taste. If placed in a stoppered jar they can be shaken together and stored ready for use. I generally keep in the store-cupboard a basic supply of sunflower oil and extra virgin olive oil.

In addition, a variety of oils and vinegars of different flavours are now readily available in many shops.

Tips

1 Buy only one variety of flavoured oil at a time because if you have too wide a choice their shelf-life may expire before you have used them all up. Look at the date stamp before buying.

2 Use strong-flavoured oils sparingly, e.g. sesame, walnut and the other nut oils; their flavour is best used to enhance the milder oils, e.g. sunflower.

3 Likewise, be sparing in your use of highly flavoured vinegars such as raspberry or green peppercorn. They can be used to enhance the flavour of wine vinegar.

4 Marry the flavour of the oil and vinegar to the ingredients in your recipe (see some ideas in Cheese, Fruit and Nut Salads, page 27).

5 For the quickest-ever vinaigrette, merely shake together 1 part balsamic vinegar and 2 parts sunflower oil. No seasonings are needed – balsamic vinegar is a matured wine vinegar, dark brown in colour, and this dressing has sufficient flavour from these two ingredients.

(*Continued overleaf.*)

6 If you prefer to leave out oil altogether, make a salad dressing with clear honey, sharpened with wine vinegar and mustard, plus chopped parsley or chives (reckon about 1 tablespoon honey to 1 teaspoon vinegar, but taste for flavour).

Orange and carrot salad

The speedy method given below uses the coarse grater on a food processor or electric mixer. If you do not possess an electric grater, you can mix coarsely grated carrots with orange juice and vinaigrette, adding some grated zest from the orange for a tangy flavour.

Serves 1–2

INGREDIENTS

1 small orange
2 carrots
vinaigrette dressing (page 29)

METHOD

1 Scrub the orange: leave the peel on half but discard the peel from the other half. Chop into chunks.
2 Grate the carrots and orange together in the electric grater.
3 Dress with vinaigrette.

Devilled toasted cheese

Serves 2

Cooking time: approximately 5 minutes

INGREDIENTS

2 large slices, or 4 small slices, wholemeal bread
a knob of soft margarine
4 oz (115 g) Cheddar cheese,* grated
4 teaspoons milk
1 teaspoon whole-grain mustard
1 teaspoon of the runny base of bottled chutney (or chutney
   sauce if you can find it)

METHOD

1 Toast the bread on one side only.
2 Mix all the other ingredients together to form a
   smooth paste.
3 Spread over the untoasted side of the bread.
4 Place under a hot grill until melted and beginning to
   bubble and brown. Serve immediately.

* Ring the changes with Double Gloucester, Wensleydale, low-fat
Cheddar or half-fat Red Leicester. (Taste the cheese first and
avoid any that are too salty in flavour.)

Fresh pasta with cheese sauce

INGREDIENTS

fresh pasta*
soft cheese with garlic and herbs or black pepper
butter
milk
sherry or Marsala
freshly grated Parmesan cheese

METHOD

1 Put a few drops of oil into a pan of rapidly boiling, slightly salted water and cook the pasta *al dente*, i.e. cooked but still slightly firm when bitten. For timing, ask advice when buying: it usually takes about 1–3 minutes but this depends on the thickness.

2 In a separate pan, melt the cheese with a knob of butter, thinning with a little milk. Add a good dash of sherry or Marsala.

3 Drain the pasta and dish up coated with the cheese sauce. Serve grated Parmesan separately.

* The most attractive kind for this dish is the green *pasta verde*. If you can only rarely find pasta freshly made, buy more than you need: it will freeze for up to a month.

Puff-pastry tarts

Tomato, cheese and mustard tart

Serves 3–4 for lunch (can be reheated for a second serving next day); or cut into a dozen or so strips for cocktail snacks

Oven temperature: 230°C, 450°F, gas mark 8

Cooking time: 20–25 minutes

You will need a non-stick or lightly greased Swiss-roll tin approximately 7 × 11 inches (18 × 28 cm).

INGREDIENTS

8 oz (225 g) ready-made puff pastry
1–1½ tablespoons mild French mustard
3 oz (85 g) grated Emmental cheese
3 medium tomatoes, thinly sliced
salt and black pepper

METHOD

1 If using frozen pastry, allow it to defrost completely. Roll out thinly on a lightly floured surface and cut to fit the tin. With a sharp knife mark out a border of ¾ inch (2 cm). Allow to rest in the refrigerator for ½ hour.
2 Spread generously with the mustard, leaving the border uncovered.

(*Continued overleaf.*)

3 Place the grated cheese over the mustard.
4 Top with the tomato and season lightly.
5 Bake for 20–25 minutes, until the sides are puffy and the base is a golden brown.
6 Serve warm. It can be lightly re-heated after cooling.

Mushroom and onion tart

Serves 3–4 for lunch

Oven temperature: 230°C, 450°F, gas mark 8

Cooking time: 20–25 minutes

You will need a non-stick or lightly greased Swiss-roll tin 7 × 11 inches (18 × 28 cm).

INGREDIENTS

8 oz (225 g) ready-made puff pastry
6–8 oz (170–225 g) mushrooms, sliced
1 small onion, sliced
1 ½ oz (45 g) butter
flour
beaten egg
salt and freshly ground black pepper

METHOD

1 If using frozen pastry, allow it to defrost completely before rolling out and cutting to fit the tin as in the previous recipe. Mark the ¾ inch (2 cm) border and refrigerate for ½ hour, as for Tomato, Cheese and Mustard Tart.

2 Meanwhile, sauté the sliced mushrooms and onion in the butter, thickening with a little flour and beaten egg, and season well. Allow to cool.

3 Spread the mushroom mixture over the pastry up to the border.

4 Bake for 20–25 minutes, until the pastry is cooked and the edge is puffy and golden brown.

Spaghetti bolognese (vegetarian)

You might find it difficult to guess that this sauce contains a breakfast cereal: it adds a pleasant texture and flavour and helps to thicken the sauce.

Serves 3

Cooking time: 25–30 minutes

INGREDIENTS

2 tablespoons oil
1 onion, chopped
2 oz (55 g) mushrooms, sliced
1 stick celery, sliced (optional)
¼ green pepper, seeded and chopped
2 tomatoes, peeled, seeded and chopped
2 tablespoons tomato purée
1 teaspoon oregano
1 clove garlic, crushed
½ pint (285 ml) stock
2 oz (55 g) All-Bran or Bran Buds cereal
salt and pepper
6 oz (170 g) spaghetti

METHOD

1 Put the oil with the chopped-up vegetables, tomato purée, oregano and garlic into a frying-pan and fry for a few minutes.

2 Stir in the stock and the bran cereal, season, cover and simmer for 25–30 minutes. Stir occasionally to prevent burning and if the sauce gets too thick add a little more stock.

3 Cook the spaghetti as instructed on the packet and serve with this vegetarian bolognese sauce.

Variations

In place of All-Bran or Bran Buds in this recipe

(*a*) substitute lentils (see the packet for cooking instructions: most varieties will soften in the sauce without pre-soaking or pre-cooking); *or*

(*b*) substitute grated raw carrot

or serve instead a basic ratatouille (see page 184) as the sauce; sprinkle with grated Parmesan cheese.

Ring the changes with different shapes of fresh pasta, e.g. tagliatelle, tagliarini. They are particularly attractive sold in the Italian flag colours of red, white and green (coloured commercially with tomato and spinach).

Stuffed courgette (or pepper) bake

This is a useful standby for vegetarians or vegans. It can also be made with halved and seeded yellow or red peppers, first parboiled for 5 minutes. The unpeeled lemon gives an exotic bitter-lemon flavour.

Serves 2

Oven temperature: 180°C, 350°F, gas mark 4

Cooking time: about 20 minutes

INGREDIENTS

1 small onion, sliced
1 tablespoon oil
½ cup rice (a mixture of wild and long-grain rice is particularly recommended)
¼ teaspoon salt
1 tablespoon raisins
1 tablespoon pine nuts or chopped nuts
¼ teaspoon ground cinnamon
3 large or 4 medium courgettes
1–2 lemons
about ½ pint (285 ml) vegetable stock (can be made from a cube)

METHOD

1 Fry the onion in the oil until softened and slightly golden.
2 Add the rice and fry for a few minutes longer.
3 Pour on ¾ cup water and add the salt; put the lid on the pan and simmer until cooked.
4 Stir in the raisins, nuts and cinnamon.
5 Cut the washed, trimmed courgettes in half lengthwise and hollow out by removing the seeds with a sharp spoon.
6 Heap the rice mixture into the hollows.
7 Place in a roasting pan on a single layer of very thinly sliced, unpeeled lemon, with vegetable stock to come a little way up the sides of the courgettes.
8 Cover the pan and bake until tender, about 20 minutes. Lift away from the lemon and liquid and serve hot.

Vegetable crumble

Serves 4–6. Can also be served cold or reheated for a second day.

Oven temperature: 180°C, 350°F, gas mark 4

Cooking time: 40–50 minutes

For speedy preparation of the vegetables use a food processor.

INGREDIENTS

1 lb (450 g) mixed vegetables, e.g. carrots, parsnips, leeks,
   courgettes
4 oz (115 g) mushrooms
¼ green pepper
14 oz (400 g) can
   tomatoes (preferably chopped)
black pepper
½ teaspoon salt
2½ oz (70 g) margarine
5 oz (140 g) wholemeal flour
2½ oz (70 g) rolled oats
2 tablespoons oil
seasoning
sunflower or sesame seeds

METHOD

1 Wash the vegetables. Peel the carrots and parsnips.
2 Steam the sliced carrots, parsnips and leeks for 10
   minutes. Or sauté in a lightly oiled wok, with the lid on.

3 Meanwhile, cut the courgettes and mushrooms into medium-thick slices and coarsely chop the de-seeded green pepper.

4 Transfer all these vegetables to a shallow baking dish and moisten with 2–3 tablespoons water or liquor from the steamer.

5 Put the canned tomatoes, with their juice, and the pepper and salt into the food processor and blend for a few seconds. If preparing by hand use a can of chopped tomatoes with their juice and season to taste. Pour over the vegetables in the dish.

6 Make a crumble: rub the margarine into the flour and seasoning, and stir in the oats and oil.

7 Cover the vegetables with the crumble mixture. Then sprinkle the surface with sunflower or sesame seeds.

8 Bake in a moderate oven for 40–50 minutes (insert a sharp-pointed knife to test the vegetables for tenderness).

Serve hot or cold.

Baked stuffed fillets of fish

Serves 2

Oven temperature: 190°C, 375°F, gas mark 5

Cooking time: 35–40 minutes

INGREDIENTS

2 plaice or lemon sole (filleted across to give 4 large fillets)
1 oz (30 g) margarine or butter
1 small onion, sliced
2 oz (55 g) mushrooms, sliced
2 tablespoons flour
¼ pint (140 ml) milk
salt and pepper
½ tablespoon chopped parsley*
1 teaspoon lemon juice
2 oz (55 g) shrimps, chopped (optional)
4 tablespoons fresh breadcrumbs*
2 tablespoons grated cheese*

METHOD

1 Grease an ovenproof casserole and put in two fillets side by side, skin side down.
2 Melt the margarine in a small saucepan and fry the onion and mushrooms until well softened.

* Store supplies of these in the freezer; they will be ready for use without the need to grate small quantities. Washed parsley, patted dry with kitchen paper, can be frozen ready for crumbling.

3 Stir in the flour and cook for a minute or two before gradually stirring in the milk. Simmer, stirring, to make a thick sauce.

4 Add seasoning, parsley, lemon juice and shrimps.

5 Pour the sauce on to each of the fillets and top with the two remaining fillets, skin side up.

6 Season and sprinkle with the breadcrumbs and cheese.

7 Bake, covered, for 35–40 minutes, uncovering to brown slightly towards the end of cooking time.

Grilled fish fillet with cheese-crumb topping

Serves 1

INGREDIENTS

1 fillet of plaice, lemon sole or other flat fish
salt and black pepper
2 tablespoons fresh breadcrumbs
2 tablespoons grated Cheddar cheese
1 tablespoon chopped parsley
grated rind of half a lemon
butter

METHOD

1 Preheat the grill to medium heat. Grease the grill rack or a shallow tin and place the fish in the centre, skin side down. Season well.
2 Mix together the breadcrumbs, cheese, parsley and lemon rind, and spread carefully over the top of the fish.
3 Dot with butter and grill for 15–20 minutes until the fish is cooked through and the topping is crisp and golden.

Pan-fried plaice with orange sauce

Serves 1

INGREDIENTS

1 large fillet of plaice
flour, seasoned with salt and pepper
1 oz (55 g) butter
juice of 1 orange

Serve with salad, e.g. a 'colour clash' of sliced tomato in vinaigrette, garnished with snipped fresh basil leaves.

METHOD

1 To bring out the fresh-caught flavour in sea fish, wash the fish and sprinkle with salt. Leave wet on a plate for a short while before patting dry and coating with seasoned flour.
2 Melt the butter in a frying-pan and when sizzling hot fry the fish on both sides. Remove and keep warm.
3 Add more butter if necessary, stir in a couple of teaspoons of seasoned flour to thicken and when just starting to colour, gradually stir in the fresh orange juice to make a sauce.
4 Pour the sauce over the fish.

Scottish salmon (grilled)

Note: the marinade and oatmeal coating protects the salmon from the fierce heat of the grill, keeping it moist.

INGREDIENTS

Per person
4 oz (115 g) Scottish salmon steak *or* 5 oz (140 g) salmon
   fillet, skinned
1 tablespoon whisky or Drambuie
1–2 tablespoons fine or medium oatmeal
salt and pepper
oil or ½ oz (15 g) melted butter

Serve with a mixed leaf salad and hot crusty bread, or steamed vegetables and potatoes.

METHOD

1 Brush the salmon with the whisky or Drambuie and leave for 10 minutes; turn over and brush again.
2 Mix the oatmeal and seasoning and coat the salmon very thoroughly, pressing on well.
3 Preheat the grill and lightly grease the grill pan.
4 Brush the coated fish lightly with oil or melted butter and grill fast for 2 minutes on each side, brushing with more oil or butter as they are turned.
5 Lower the heat to medium and grill for a further 2–3 minutes on each side, depending on the thickness, until just cooked: the thickest part should be firm but cooked and pale pink when pierced with a knife.

Tuna avocado bake

Serves 2

Oven temperature: 200°C, 400°F, gas mark 6 (or cook gently under a low–medium grill)

Cooking time: approximately 20–25 minutes

INGREDIENTS

mayonnaise
curry paste and/or mango chutney
1 ripe avocado (halved and stoned)
1 can (100 g) tuna in vegetable oil

METHOD

1 Flavour a good-quality mayonnaise with a little curry paste (the tip of a teaspoon may be sufficient), and/or add chutney to taste.
2 Scoop out the avocado flesh, leaving just enough behind to keep the skin firm.
3 Mash the well-drained tuna with the flavoured mayonnaise and avocado, and stuff into the avocado skins.
4 Bake or grill gently until heated right through.

Variation

This recipe can also be served uncooked.

Chicken with apricot sauce

This can be cooked on top of the stove or in the oven; or, following the manufacturer's instructions, it can be cooked in the microwave.

Serves 2 or more

Oven temperature: 200°C, 400°F, gas mark 6

Cooking time: 40 minutes in the oven *or* 30 minutes on top of the stove *or* 20 minutes in the microwave

INGREDIENTS

1 can (400 g) *unsweetened* apricots
2 tablespoons packet French onion soup (used dry)
2 or more chicken portions
½ tablespoon chutney

Serve with Couscous (see page 178) *or* plain boiled rice.

METHOD

1 In a blender, whisk together the apricots and juice with 2 tablespoons dry soup powder.
2 Bake, simmer or microwave the chicken in this sauce, stirring occasionally and adding a little stock or water if necessary to prevent burning. The pan or casserole needs to be covered.
3 When tender, stir in the chutney, tasting for flavour.

Crisp spiced chicken

Oven temperature: 220°C, 425°F, gas mark 7

Cooking time: 30–35 minutes

INGREDIENTS

chicken portions
cooking oil

Per portion
2 tablespoons Bran Flakes finely crushed and mixed with a
  generous pinch each of ground coriander, ground cumin,
  garlic salt, tandoori spice

METHOD

1 Wash or wipe and dry the chicken and brush lightly
  with oil.
2 Dip into the crushed, spiced Bran Flakes, pressing
  them on to coat the chicken portions.
3 Place on an oiled baking dish and bake for 30–35
  minutes until crisped, browned and cooked right
  through.

Herbed chicken (low fat)

Note: for parties this can be bulk-cooked in a roaster bag, cooled rapidly and served cold. The cold chicken is also convenient for picnics.

Oven temperature: 180°C, 350°F, gas mark 4

Cooking time: approximately 20–30 minutes (or see instructions with roaster bags)

INGREDIENTS

boneless skinned chicken breasts
salt and pepper
mixed dried herbs

METHOD

1 Wash or wipe the chicken and pat dry.
2 Season, and then sprinkle with 3 generous pinches of mixed dried herbs on each side of each chicken breast.
3 Bake uncovered in a lightly greased non-stick pan. *Or* follow directions given with roaster bags (e.g. shake a teaspoon of flour into the bag, insert the chicken and seal with the tie provided. Slit the bag to allow some air to escape and then roast for approximately 20–30 minutes, depending on the thickness).
4 Serve hot, with steamed vegetables. Or cool quickly and serve with salad and Cranberry and Marmalade Sauce (page 25).

Gammon steak with apple and spiced cider

Serves 1–2

INGREDIENTS

¼ pint (140 ml) medium-sweet cider
1 tablespoon demerara sugar
2 generous pinches ground cinnamon
2 generous pinches nutmeg
½ medium cooking apple, peeled and sliced
1–2 gammon steaks
cooking oil
pepper

Can be served with potatoes and swedes or sprouts.

METHOD

1 Place the cider in a saucepan with the sugar and spices and heat gently to dissolve the sugar.
2 Add the apple, and simmer gently until it is soft and the cider is almost absorbed (about 10 minutes).
3 Meanwhile, trim the rind from the gammon steaks and snip the fat at intervals. Brush one side with oil and sprinkle with pepper. Place on a grill rack, put under a fairly hot grill and cook for 5 minutes.
4 Turn the gammon, brush with more oil, sprinkle with pepper and cook for a further 5 minutes.
5 Transfer to a hot serving dish and spoon the apple mixture on top.

Beef and mushrooms in sour cream

This is an economical version of a beef strogonoff because it uses cubes of slow-cooked stewing steak instead of the more expensive strips of fillet steak.

Serves 2 (the meat, onion and mushrooms should be doubled for 4 servings, but there is no need to double the rest of the ingredients, because there is plenty of sauce)

INGREDIENTS

½ oz (15 g) butter
12 oz (340 g) stewing steak, cubed
1 small onion, diced
salt and pepper
4 oz (115 g) button mushrooms, wiped and cut in quarters
3 level tablespoons flour
1 tablespoon lemon juice
about 5 fl oz (140 ml) sour cream
1 tablespoon chopped parsley

Garnish with parsley and serve with rice, noodles or new potatoes (or with thick crusty bread to mop up the sauce).

METHOD

1 Melt the butter in a large pan, add the steak and onion, and fry for about 10 minutes. Add seasonings and ¼ pint (140 ml) water, and bring to the boil. Cover and simmer for approximately 1½ hours until the meat is tender.

2 Add the mushrooms and cook for a further 10 minutes.

3 Blend the flour with 4 tablespoons water and stir into the pan. Continue heating until thickened.

4 Stir in the lemon juice, and when almost boiling add the sour cream and parsley. Heat again gently, but do not allow to boil.

5 Taste for flavour and adjust seasoning if necessary.

Pork chops in rosemary, orange and pepper sauce

Serves 2; for 4 servings, buy 4 chops but make the same amount of sauce

INGREDIENTS

2 trimmed loin pork chops
salt and pepper
1 oz (30 g) demerara sugar
1 oz (30 g) butter or margarine
1 clove garlic, peeled and sliced
1 oz (30 g) cornflour
½ level teaspoon dried rosemary
3 tablespoons lemon juice
3 tablespoons orange juice
½ green pepper, de-seeded and chopped
4–8 slices fresh orange

Serve with rice and a green vegetable.

METHOD

1 Season the chops with salt, pepper and a little of the sugar. Fry in the butter or margarine with the garlic until browned. Remove the chops and discard the garlic.
2 Add the rest of the sugar and the cornflour and rosemary to the drippings. Stir; gradually add ½ pint (285 ml) water. Cook, stirring, until glossy.

3 Add the fruit juices and green pepper. Return chops
  to the pan and place a slice of orange on each chop.
4 Cover and simmer for 40 minutes until tender, basting
  occasionally; uncover for the last 10 minutes.
5 Garnish with the remaining slices of orange.

Lamb chops with peach chutney

Serves 2

INGREDIENTS

2 lamb chops (chump, loin, or lamb steaks cut from the leg)
cooking oil
salt and black pepper
2–4 teaspoons peach chutney (depending on size of chops)

Serve with cooked vegetables or salad.

METHOD

1 Brush the chops with oil, season and grill on one side
  under high heat until beginning to brown. Reduce
  the heat to moderate and continue cooking through.
2 Turn, and repeat on the other side until almost
  cooked.
3 Spread the chutney on top and continue to heat
  under a moderate grill until hot and thoroughly
  cooked (test with a skewer or pointed knife: the juices
  should be clear rather than pink).

Stir fry

This recipe borrows from the Chinese art of stir fry, and uses up leftover cooked meat or poultry.

Serves 2 or more

INGREDIENTS

1 tablespoon oil
raw vegetables
  onion or spring onion (thinly sliced)
  hard vegetables, e.g. leek, carrot, pepper (cut in thin slices or strips), baby corn
  tender vegetables (thinly sliced), e.g. cabbage, Chinese leaves, mushrooms, green beans, mange-touts, bean sprouts
  frozen vegetables – use these if your stock of fresh vegetables lacks variety (blanch or lightly cook in boiling water)
strips of cooked meat or poultry
stock
flavouring, e.g. soy sauce, peach chutney, tomato ketchup

METHOD

1 Heat the oil in a large frying-pan or wok, fry the onion and hard vegetables until they begin to soften.
2 Then add the tender vegetables that take longest to cook, using sliced cabbage to give bulk to this dish.
3 When these vegetables are becoming tender, stir in the meat or poultry to heat through thoroughly.
4 Add the frozen vegetables, and the rest of the tender vegetables such as bean sprouts and mange-touts.

5 Pour on sufficient stock and flavouring to moisten. Stir rapidly without any lid, allowing some of the moisture to evaporate.

6 Serve piping hot.

Veal escalope (low fat)

Serves 1

INGREDIENTS

1 escalope of veal
lemon juice
salt and freshly ground black pepper
dried or fresh rosemary *or* dried or fresh sage

Serve with steamed vegetables.

METHOD

1 Wash and dry the veal and, if necessary, beat it with a rolling-pin to tenderize it and make sure it is thin.

2 Sprinkle both sides generously with lemon juice and season lightly with salt and pepper.

3 *Either* sprinkle both sides with the chosen dried herb *or* lay a sprig of the fresh herb under and on top of the veal.

4 Cook under a hot grill for about 3 minutes on each side.

Avocado with pink grapefruit juice

Serves 2

INGREDIENTS

1 ripe avocado
granulated sugar
½ pink grapefruit *

METHOD

1 Halve the avocado, remove the stone.
2 Sprinkle the hollows with granulated sugar.
3 Squeeze the juice from the grapefruit and pour into the sugar, allowing the juice to overflow on to the cut surface of the avocado.

* For those who like a sharper flavour, substitute the juice of white grapefruit or lemon.

Crunchy apple and nut creams

This is an excellent standby for last-minute entertaining: it can be made just before your guests arrive. Or it can be kept for a few hours in the refrigerator, although sometimes the juice from the apple weeps a little; this does not seem to matter in small ramekins.

Serves 2

INGREDIENTS

2 tablespoons stiffly whipped double or whipping cream
2 tablespoons low-calorie plain yogurt
1 dessert apple*
1 tablespoon mixed grated or chopped nuts (or grated hazelnuts)
1 tablespoon lemon juice
honey to sweeten (optional)
demerara sugar

METHOD

1 Beat the whipped cream and yogurt together.
2 Grate the unpeeled apple finely so that it is mushy.
3 Stir the apple, nuts and lemon juice into the cream mixture and sweeten (if necessary) with honey.
4 Transfer to a bowl or ramekins. Cover with a thick layer of demerara sugar and place in the refrigerator.

* For preference, choose a firm, white-fleshed variety like Granny Smith.

Hot orange dessert

Serves 2

INGREDIENTS

1 cup sugar
2 oranges
4–6 maraschino cherries
1–2 tablespoons Cointreau or other orange-flavoured
   liqueur
1 tablespoon maraschino juice from the jar

METHOD

1 In a small pan without a lid bring the sugar and
  1 cup of water to the boil, stirring to dissolve. Boil
  gently for a further 5 minutes.
2 Meanwhile, grate the rind from 1 orange, then peel
  the oranges, discarding all the pith. Cut the flesh
  across into very thin (¼ inch, ½ cm) slices, and cut
  each slice into 3 or 4 segments. Cut up the cherries.
3 Remove the syrup from the heat and add the grated
  orange rind, liqueur and maraschino juice.
4 When ready to serve, heat deep soup or dessert
  plates. Bring the syrup to the boil again and pour it
  over the oranges and cherries on the plates. Serve
  immediately.

Minted melon with raspberries or orange

Serves 2

INGREDIENTS

1 small melon
caster sugar (optional)
a few sprigs of fresh mint
1 small carton fresh raspberries *or* 1 large orange

METHOD

1 Cut the melon crosswise in half and scoop out the seeds.
2 If you have a sweet tooth, sprinkle the melon halves with caster sugar.
3 With scissors, snip plenty of fresh mint into the scooped-out hollow and around the surface of each half melon.
4 Fill the centre with fresh raspberries, or fresh orange cut into segments free from membrane. Decorate with a small sprig of mint.

Pears in red wine

Pears in Red Wine is an excellent standby freezer dish. I generally replace them as soon as they are used so that there is a ready-cooked dessert in the house. They keep a good flavour and texture if defrosted overnight in the refrigerator or for a few hours at room temperature.

Serves 4, hot or cold – any not required immediately can be frozen

INGREDIENTS

¼ pint (140 ml) red wine
3 oz (85 g) sugar
½ cinnamon stick
strip of lemon rind
4 medium-sized firm eating pears*

Can be served with single cream or toasted flaked almonds.

METHOD

1 In a deep saucepan large enough to take all the pears standing upright, place the wine, ¼ pint (140 ml) water, sugar, cinnamon and lemon rind. Bring slowly to the boil, stirring to dissolve the sugar.
2 Meanwhile, peel the pears thinly, leaving them whole

* Choose a squat rather than a long shape for ease of fitting in the saucepan.

with the stalks on. Cut a thin slice from the base so
that they will stand upright in the syrup.
3 Put the lid on the pan and simmer gently until
tender, approximately 20–30 minutes. Baste and turn
occasionally.
4 Remove the pears.
5 Boil the syrup briskly for a few minutes, uncovered,
to reduce it and make it more syrupy. Discard the
cinnamon stick.
6 Serve the pears, hot or cold, surrounded by the syrup
or place in a rigid container, pour the syrup over,
cool and freeze.

Summer fruit crumble

On an overcast summer day, this makes a warm alternative to a cold Summer Pudding (page 110).

Serves 3

Oven temperature: 180°C, 350°F, gas mark 4

Cooking time: 30 minutes

INGREDIENTS

8 oz (225 g) mixed summer fruits, e.g. raspberries, black-currants, redcurrants, strawberries (fresh or frozen), lightly stewed
4 oz (115 g) apple purée (made from fresh stewed apples or use a can)
sugar

Crumble mix
2 oz (55 g) flour
1 ½ oz (45 g) porridge oats
1 ½ oz (45 g) margarine
1 ½ oz (45 g) sugar (preferably golden granulated)

Serve with fromage frais, yogurt or ice-cream.

METHOD

1 Place the lightly stewed fruit and apple purée, sweetened to taste, in an ovenproof dish.
2 Mix flour and oats. Rub in margarine. Stir in sugar. Sprinkle this crumble thickly over the fruit.
3 Bake for 30 minutes. Serve warm.

Yorkshire rhubarb crisp

Serves 4

Oven temperature: 180°C, 350°F, gas mark 4

Cooking time: 35 minutes

INGREDIENTS

1 lb (450 g) rhubarb
2 tablespoons golden syrup
grated rind and juice of an orange
2 oz (55 g) demerara sugar
2 oz (55 g) butter, melted
6 oz (170 g) breadcrumbs
2 oz (55 g) golden granulated or demerara sugar

METHOD

1 Cut the rhubarb into 1 inch (2.5 cm) pieces. If using the tender early variety, place it in a 2 pint (1.1 litre) ovenproof dish. If using the later, thicker sticks, pour boiling water over them and leave to soak for 10 minutes before draining and replacing in the dish.
2 Pour the syrup, 1 tablespoon water, orange rind, juice and demerara sugar over the fruit and stir to mix.
3 Melt the butter in a pan and stir in the breadcrumbs and golden granulated or demerara sugar. Sprinkle thickly on top of the rhubarb.
4 Bake in a moderate oven for 35 minutes.

Instant iced coffee shake

INGREDIENTS

For each serving
¼ pint (140 ml) semi-skimmed milk
1 heaped teaspoon instant coffee granules
1 teaspoon sugar (optional)
1 ice cube
scoop of ice-cream (coffee, chocolate or vanilla)

METHOD

1 Place milk, coffee, sugar (only if you have a sweet
  tooth) and ice cube into a liquidizer. Do not fill more
  than two thirds full because the volume increases.
  Blend at maximum speed for 1 minute.
2 Pour into tall glasses, topped with a scoop of ice-
  cream. Serve with a straw for drinking and a long
  spoon for eating the ice-cream.

Chapter Three
Favourite Recipes Remembered

SOUPS AND APPETIZERS

Farmhouse vegetable soup
Liver pâté
Lentil and bacon soup

VEGETABLES

Brussels sprouts and chestnuts
Bubble and squeak
Mashed potatoes and swede
   with horseradish cream
   with orange
Rice and potatoes

FISH

Baked 'fried' fish
Soused mackerel

MEAT

Boiled beef and carrots
   herb dumplings
   hot salt-beef sandwiches
   left-over salt beef
Chicken liver florentine
   chicken livers on toast
Cornish pasties
Meat loaf
Shepherd's pie (using cooked meat)
Steak and kidney puddings (suet-topped)
Toad in the hole

DESSERTS

Bread and butter pudding (lower fat)
Caramel custard
Fruit cobbler
Lemon meringue sponge
Pancakes
St Clement's pancakes
Plum and apple crumble
Rice pudding (made with semi-skimmed milk)
Spotted Dick
Summer puddings
Semolina pudding (made with semi-skimmed milk)

Farmhouse vegetable soup

Serves 2–3

INGREDIENTS

knob of margarine
1 onion, peeled and chopped
2 rashers bacon, de-rinded and chopped
1 small turnip, peeled and diced
1 small parsnip, peeled and diced
1 small leek, sliced
1/2 tablespoon tomato purée
1 1/4 pints (0.7 litre) stock
1/2 oz (15 g) pearl barley
1/4–1/2 small green cabbage, shredded
salt and ground black pepper
chopped parsley to garnish

METHOD

1 Melt the margarine in a large pan and sauté the
  onion and bacon for 5 minutes, until softened.
2 Add remaining vegetables, except cabbage, and sauté
  for 5 minutes. Add tomato purée, stock and pearl
  barley and stir well.
3 Bring to the boil and simmer for about 15 minutes
  until vegetables are really tender.
4 Add cabbage and cook for a further 3–4 minutes.
  Season to taste. Serve garnished with chopped parsley.

Liver pâté

There are a number of recipes for liver pâté, some of them adding brandy or herbs, some of them more complicated and needing to be cooked in a terrine. But this is the easy, basic recipe handed down from mother to daughter in my family. It was made using a mincer, but nowadays I find it quicker (and easier to wash up) using a food processor.

Serve as an appetizer with water biscuits or triangles of toast.

INGREDIENTS

1 small onion, peeled and sliced
chicken fat or soft white cooking fat
8 oz (225 g) chicken livers*
salt and pepper
2 eggs, hard-boiled
a little stale bread (if using a mincer)

METHOD

1 Fry the onion in the fat until softened. Remove the onion to the mincer or food processor.
2 Wash and dry the livers, season with salt and pepper, and fry until browned on the outside but still slightly pink inside.

* If frozen, defrost thoroughly before use.

3 Mince or process together the onion, livers and one hard-boiled egg, with enough of the melted fat to make a soft consistency. If using a mincer, clear out all the mixture by mincing through some stale bread.

4 Taste for seasoning. Spread in a shallow dish, cool and refrigerate for a few hours until needed.*

5 Decorate with hard-boiled egg yolk, pressed through a sieve, surrounded by the finely chopped egg white.

* At this stage it can be frozen in small containers. Defrost thoroughly before use.

Lentil and bacon soup

Serves 3 as a main course

INGREDIENTS

3 oz (85 g) red lentils
1 ½ pints (0.9 litre) chicken stock
½ garlic clove, crushed
1 clove
3–4 oz (85–115 g) lean bacon rashers, de-rinded and diced
8 oz (225 g) canned tomatoes, preferably chopped
1 small or ½ medium onion, chopped
pepper
8 oz (225 g) potatoes, peeled and diced
1 tablespoon lemon juice
to garnish: crispy fried bacon rolls, chopped fresh parsley,
    grated cheese or croûtons

METHOD

1 Wash the lentils and put them in a saucepan with the
   stock. Add the garlic, clove, bacon, tomatoes, onion
   and season with pepper.
2 Bring to the boil, cover and simmer for about 1 hour
   until the lentils are soft.
3 Add the potatoes and cook for a further 20 minutes
   until tender. Remove the clove. *

* Omit step 4 if you prefer the soup unpuréed.

4 Allow the soup to cool slightly and then purée in a blender or food processor for a smooth soup. Return the soup to the pan.

5 Add the lemon juice and reheat gently. Adjust the seasoning to taste and garnish just before serving.

Brussels sprouts and chestnuts

I well remember the chore of boiling and peeling chestnuts: trying to avoid scalding fingers while attempting to keep the kernels whole. Nowadays, canned or dried chestnuts make the preparation easy.

Serves 2

INGREDIENTS

2 tablespoons canned whole chestnuts in brine *or* dried
   chestnuts boiled in water to soften
knob of butter or margarine
½ lb (225 g) Brussels sprouts, trimmed, halved and washed
chicken stock

METHOD

1 Drain the chestnuts and chop into quarters.
2 In a saucepan, fry the chestnuts lightly in the fat.
3 Add the sprouts with a little chicken stock and boil until just tender. Uncover the pan for the last few minutes to evaporate off most of the stock.

Bubble and squeak

To make a change from the usual potato and cabbage mixture, this recipe substitutes Brussels sprouts. The grated cheese gives a crisp savoury topping.

Serves 4

Oven temperature: 200°C, 400°F, gas mark 6

Cooking time: 30–40 minutes after preliminary cooking

For freezing, a foil casserole is recommended.

INGREDIENTS

1½ lb (0.7 kg) old-crop potatoes, peeled
½ lb (225 g) Brussels sprouts, halved and finely sliced
3 tablespoons milk
1 oz (30 g) butter
salt and black pepper
3 oz (85 g) Cheddar cheese, grated

METHOD

1 Steam or boil the potatoes until soft.
2 Steam the Brussels sprouts for about 5 minutes, until cooked but still slightly crisp.
3 Mash the potatoes smoothly with the milk and butter, seasoning well.
4 Combine the potatoes with the sprouts. Taste again for seasoning.
5 Transfer to an oiled baking dish; press down and mark with a fork.
6 Sprinkle the grated cheese over the top.

7 Bake for 30–40 minutes, until hot and evenly browned.

8 After step 7 it can be served immediately or frozen for future use. Before freezing, cool, cover with foil, seal into a freezer bag and label. To use: thaw overnight in the refrigerator, or at room temperature for 3–4 hours. Reheat in a hot oven for about 30 minutes, until heated through.

Mashed potatoes and swede

Serves 1

INGREDIENTS

5 oz (140 g) potato (variety suitable for mashing)
5 oz (140 g) swede
knob of butter
milk
salt, pepper and nutmeg

For serving with steak or other beef dish
1–2 teaspoons horseradish cream

For serving with lamb
grated rind and juice of ¼–½ orange

METHOD

1 Peel and cut up the vegetables, and boil until soft in lightly salted water. Drain and mash with butter, add a little milk to soften if necessary. Season to taste with salt, pepper and nutmeg.

2 Flavour well with horseradish or orange.

Rice and potatoes

I remember this as one of my mother's family recipes.

Serves 2

Oven temperature: 190°C, 375°F, gas mark 5

Cooking time: approximately 45 minutes to 1 hour

INGREDIENTS

1 medium potato (long rather than round in shape)
2–3 tablespoons long-grain rice, washed and drained
½ small onion, sliced
salt and pepper
½ oz (15 g) dripping or butter

You will need a small (½ pint) casserole dish, well greased with extra butter.

METHOD

1 Peel the potato and slice thickly (¾ in, 2 cm).
2 Put the rice and about 2½ fl oz (70 ml) boiling water into the casserole, scatter in the onion and season with a little salt. Arrange the potato on top of the rice, season with salt and pepper and dot with some of the butter or dripping.
3 Bake uncovered in the oven.
4 Add a little more boiling water after 20–30 minutes, and brush the potatoes with more dripping or butter, baking until they become soft on the inside and crisp and browned on the surface.

Baked 'fried' fish

This has a similar taste to ordinary fried fish, but the kitchen smells are minimized by baking it in the oven.

Serves 3–4

Oven temperature: 220°C, 425°F, gas mark 7

Cooking time: approximately 20 minutes

You will need a greased baking tray.

INGREDIENTS

1 egg beaten with 3 tablespoons oil
8 oz (225 g) dried breadcrumbs or medium matzo meal
paprika, salt and pepper
6–8 small fillets of white fish

METHOD

1 In a shallow soup plate beat the egg with the oil.
2 In a second plate mix the breadcrumbs or matzo meal with seasoning.
3 Dip the fish into the egg/oil, lift up to drain slightly, and then coat with the breadcrumbs or meal, pressing lightly to cover.
4 Bake on the greased baking tray for 20 minutes, until golden and cooked.

Soused mackerel

Note: although some people leave the fish whole, I prefer to have them split, with the backbone removed (see page 186, footnote).

Serves 2

Oven temperature: 180°C, 350°F, gas mark 4

Cooking time: about 1 hour

INGREDIENTS

2 mackerel
1 bay leaf
10 peppercorns
½ small onion, sliced
pinch of salt
¼ pint (140 ml) vinegar
6 cloves
1 teaspoon muscovado sugar (optional)

METHOD

1 Halve the boned mackerel lengthwise, roll up towards the tail and secure with wooden cocktail sticks.
2 Place in a baking dish with the rest of the ingredients and ¼ pint (140 ml) water, cover and bake for about 1 hour.
3 Leave to cool in the liquor.

Note: the same recipe can be used for herrings.

Boiled beef and carrots

Serves 4 hot portions; the other 4 portions can be cooled, thinly sliced and frozen in usable quantities.

Cooking time: about 2½ hours

Serve with Herb Dumplings (see page 80).

INGREDIENTS

4 lb (1.8 kg) salt brisket, boned, rolled and tied to shape*
1 teaspoon demerara sugar
1 bay leaf
8–10 peppercorns
5 medium onions, peeled
3–4 cloves
6 large carrots, peeled
4 sticks of celery
2 turnips, peeled
2 large parsnips, peeled

METHOD

1 Put the meat into a large saucepan and cover with tepid water. Bring to the boil and skim.

(*Continued overleaf.*)

* Many butchers have their own recipe for brining beef and it may be advisable to place an order for the day and weight required, mentioning that you need a cut without excess fat. Also say whether you prefer it mild or well brined. If you buy over the counter and find the shop's recipe too salty for your taste, throw away the water once it has come to the boil, cover with more tepid water and begin again.

2 Now add the sugar, bay leaf and peppercorns, and
   1 peeled onion stuck with the cloves. Simmer gently
   for 1 hour.
3 Prepare the vegetables: leave the onions whole and
   cut the other vegetables into 2–3 pieces. Add to the
   pan and bring back to the boil. Lower the heat and
   simmer for a further 30 minutes. (If necessary, use a
   second pan – with some of the cooking liquor topped
   up with boiling water – for some of the vegetables
   and dumplings.)
4 Make the dumplings (see below), add to the pan and
   continue to simmer until the dumplings are cooked.

Herb dumplings

Makes 8

INGREDIENTS

4 oz (115 g) self-raising flour
pinch of salt
2 oz (55 g) shredded beef suet
1 level teaspoon mixed herbs

METHOD

1 Sieve the flour and salt, stir in the suet and herbs and
   mix with sufficient cold water to make a soft dough.
2 Divide into 8, and drop into the boiling liquor in the
   pan.
3 Replace the lid and continue simmering for 25–30
   minutes, turning once, until light, well risen and
   fluffy.

Hot salt-beef sandwiches

The frozen slices are particularly good *defrosted* and
then placed in a colander, balanced over a pan of
boiling water, with the lid of the pan covering the meat
in the colander. Steam until well heated through. Immediately, make into sandwiches with rye bread spread
with mustard. Serve these hot salt-beef sandwiches with
pickled cucumber.

Alternative ideas for using left-over salt beef

Hot
Steam the salt-beef slices, as above. Serve with:
    Leeks in Cheese Sauce (page 20)
    Mashed Potatoes and Swede (page 75)
    Danish Red Cabbage (page 180)

Cold
Serve cold salt-beef slices with a salad and jacket or sauté
potatoes. Add shop-bought beetroot and horseradish or a
home-made relish, such as:
    Beetroot and Orange (page 283)
    Preserved Orange Slices (page 335)
    Pickled Prunes (page 336)

Chicken liver florentine

This recipe does involve quite a lot of washing up but in my opinion it is well worth it!

Serves 2

Oven temperature: 180°C, 350°F, gas mark 4

Cooking time: after preliminary cooking, 30 minutes in the oven to brown

INGREDIENTS

1 small packet (10.6 oz, 300 g) frozen leaf spinach
1 onion, sliced
chicken fat or white cooking fat for frying
8 oz (225 g) chicken livers*
½ pint (285 ml) semi-skimmed milk
1 oz (30 g) flour
1 oz (30 g) margarine
3 heaped tablespoons grated cheese (preferably Red
   Leicester)

METHOD

1 Cook the spinach and drain well.
2 Fry the onion, lift away from the fat, and transfer to a small ovenproof casserole with the spinach.
3 Add the chicken livers to the fat left in the pan and fry lightly until sealed on the outside and still slightly pink inside.

* If frozen, defrost thoroughly before use.

4 Make a sauce from the milk, flour and margarine. (For a speedy, all-in-one method see page 20.) Stir in 2 tablespoons of the cheese.

5 Place the chicken livers on the spinach and onion, and pour the cheese sauce over the top. Sprinkle with the final tablespoon of grated cheese.

6 Bake uncovered for about 30 minutes until hot and beginning to brown.

Chicken livers on toast

Cut the livers into bite-size pieces and coat with flour seasoned with salt, black pepper and herbs. Fry briskly in a little hot oil until crisp and brown on the outside and still slightly pink inside. Pour off remaining oil and stir the livers with a squeeze of fresh lime juice or a dash of sweet sherry, marsala or red wine. Serve hot on toast as a starter or light snack.

Cornish pasties

Can be eaten hot or cold. The pastry is traditionally firm so that the pasties can be transported without crumbling.

Serves 4–6, according to size

Oven temperature: 220°C, 425°F, gas mark 7 for 15 minutes; reduced to 170°C, 325°F, gas mark 3 for 50–60 minutes

INGREDIENTS

Pastry
3 oz (85 g) lard
3 oz (85 g) block margarine
12 oz (340 g) plain flour
¼ teaspoon salt

Filling
12 oz (340 g) good quality braising steak
3 oz (85 g) turnip
3 oz (85 g) potato
3 oz (85 g) onion
salt and pepper

METHOD

1 Make shortcrust pastry by rubbing the cut-up fats into the flour and salt until the mixture resembles fresh breadcrumbs.

   Sprinkle water over the surface (approximately 4–5 tablespoons – the amount used will vary with the type of flour). Stir it with a round-bladed knife and gather it together with one hand. Knead lightly for a few moments to make a smooth dough.

    Put aside for 15 minutes or so to rest.

2 Divide the pastry into four and roll to rounds of 7–8 inches (18–20 cm) in diameter. Trim around the rim of a 7–8 inch (18–20 cm) plate. (Six smaller pasties can be made by using a 6 inch (15 cm) plate.)

3 Mix the finely diced filling ingredients together, seasoning well. Pile in the centre of the pastry rounds, damp the edges with water and draw up to the centre, pressing into a seam and fluting the edges (see illustration).

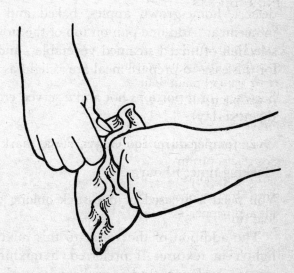

4 Place on a baking sheet, bake at 220°C, 425°F, gas mark 7 for 15 minutes to brown the pastry, then lower the heat and continue cooking for 50–60 minutes, according to size.

Meat loaf

It is a joy to have reached the age when my grown-up daughters and sons-in-law come round for a relaxed supper and then insist on doing the washing up before they go home. But I get strict instructions: the meal must not produce too many greasy pans.

This meat loaf recipe is a favourite: only one pan to wash up, and that is a non-stick loaf pan. The oven temperature and timing is right for other family favourites: small baked potatoes in their jackets and, for dessert, home-grown apples, baked and stuffed with mincemeat. Add one pan on top of the stove for a large selection of mixed steamed vegetables, and my labours for this easy-to-prepare meal are as light as theirs!

Serves 4 (or 2 portions hot and 2 served cold with salad the next day)

Oven temperature: 190°C, 375°F, gas mark 5

Cooking time: 1 hour

You need a greased or non-stick oblong 2 lb (0.9 kg) loaf tin.

The addition of the water to this mixture makes it lighter in texture. If preferred, a mixture of minced meats – beef, pork and/or veal can be used.

INGREDIENTS

1 large or 2 small eggs
1 ½ lb (680 g) minced beef
4 tablespoons porridge oats
1–2 tablespoons pickle
1 onion, finely chopped (optional)
1 tablespoon chopped parsley
salt and pepper
1 teaspoon made mustard

METHOD

1 Lightly beat the eggs in a large bowl.
2 Using a fork, mix all the rest of the ingredients into the eggs with 6 tablespoons cold water.*
3 Pack the mixture into the tin.
4 Bake for 1 hour until browned on top and cooked right through. (It will begin to come away from the sides of the tin.)

* Note: the uncooked mixture can be frozen at this stage. Pack it into a tin lined with strong foil. Fold the foil over the top of the meat, place in the freezer. When frozen, remove the foil wrapped loaf from the tin and put in a freezer bag, seal and return to the freezer.

To serve, unwrap the frozen loaf, return to the greased tin, cover and thaw overnight in the refrigerator. Bake, lightly covered, at 190°C, 375°F, gas mark 5 for 1 hour.

Shepherd's pie (using cooked meat)

For a recipe using fresh mince see page 126.

Serves 3–4

Temperature: 220°C, 425°F, gas mark 7

Cooking time: about 30 minutes

INGREDIENTS

12–16 oz (340–450 g) cooked lamb
1 onion, peeled and chopped
1 tablespoon Branston pickle
1 tablespoon chopped parsley *or* ½ teaspoon dried herbs
1 small teaspoon Marmite in a large cup of boiling water
3–4 fresh tomatoes, peeled and sliced
1 ½ lb (0.7 kg) potatoes, cooked and mashed with salt and
    pepper, milk and butter
a little butter or margarine

METHOD

1 Put the cooked lamb through a mincer.
2 Fry the onion until softened and golden.
3 In a casserole, mix the meat and onion with the pickle and herbs and moisten well with the Marmite stock, adding more water if necessary to make a soft consistency.
4 Cover with a layer of sliced tomatoes.
5 Fork on a thick layer of mashed potato, dot with butter or margarine and bake for 30 minutes until hot, with the potato beginning to brown.

Steak and kidney puddings (suet-topped)

Can be prepared in two stages. I like to get the meat prepared and cooked in advance so that the puddings only need to be topped with the suet pastry and thoroughly steamed before dinner. As long as it is promptly cooled and refrigerated, it can even be prepared one day in advance.

You will need a 1 ½ pint (0.9 litre) boilable plastic or china pudding basin *or* 3 × ½ pint (285 ml) individual pudding basins.

INGREDIENTS

1 lb (450 g) lean stewing steak
8 oz (225 g) ox kidney
2 level tablespoons flour
salt and black pepper
1 onion, peeled and chopped
about 10 fl oz (285 ml) stock

Suet-crust pastry
4 oz (115 g) self-raising flour
¼ teaspoon salt
½ teaspoon baking powder
2 oz (55 g) shredded suet

(*See over for method.*)

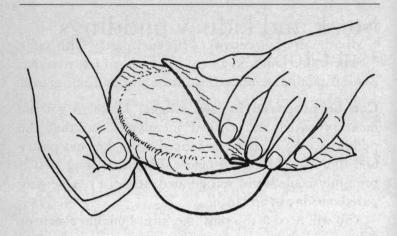

METHOD

Stage 1

1 Cut the steak into 1 inch (2.5 cm) cubes; remove the skin and core from the kidneys, and cut them into slices.
2 Coat with flour seasoned well with pepper and salt.
3 Place the meat, kidney, onion and stock into a saucepan, bring to the boil and simmer slowly for 2–2½ hours (stirring occasionally and adding a little more stock if necessary) until tender.*
4 Cool quickly (stand the pan in a sink of cold water). Spoon the cooled mixture into the pudding basins and leave refrigerated until evening, or overnight.

---

* This stage can be speeded up by using a pressure cooker, with the timing, amount of liquid and pressure according to manufacturer's instructions.

Stage 2

5 Mix the dry ingredients of the suet pastry with sufficient water (approximately 2½ fl oz, 70 ml) to make
   a soft pliable dough; knead it lightly and pat or roll
   into rounds to fit the tops of the basins.
6 Cover with greased foil, pleated to allow for expansion (see illustration).*
7 Steam for 1½ hours.

* **After step 6 the made-up puddings can be sealed in a
freezer bag and put in the freezer**. To serve, thaw overnight in
the refrigerator. When completely thawed, re-cover if necessary
with fresh greased, pleated foil and steam for 1½ hours.

Toad in the hole

The addition of apple and onion to this dish gives a new flavour to an old favourite.

Serves 2

Oven temperature: 220°C, 425°F, gas mark 7

Cooking time: 30–35 minutes, after preliminary frying

INGREDIENTS

1 medium onion, peeled and sliced
half a large cooking apple, peeled and sliced
about 2 tablespoons lard or cooking oil
8 oz (225 g) sausages*

Batter
2 oz (55 g) plain flour
¼ level teaspoon salt
1 small egg
¼ pint (140 ml) milk and water

METHOD

1 Lightly fry the sliced onion and apple in a tablespoon of lard or cooking oil. Drain from the fat and put to one side.

---

* Use beef or pork, or look for the new types of sausage sold by some specialist butchers, e.g. beef and horseradish, lamb and mint, organic meat sausages.

2 Adding a little more fat if necessary, fry the sausages over low–medium heat until they are well browned all over.

3 Meanwhile, make the batter.

If using a liquidizer, whiz all the batter ingredients except flour at maximum speed for a few seconds, add the flour in tablespoons and continue to blend for a further 30 seconds.

If making by hand, sieve the flour and salt into a bowl, make a well in the centre, add the egg and half the liquid, gradually stir in the flour and beat with a wooden spoon till smooth and 'plopping'. Gently stir in the remaining liquid.

4 Place a tablespoon of lard or cooking oil in a small baking dish or Yorkshire pudding tin, and when it is piping hot quickly add the sausages, onion and apple and pour the batter mixture over.

5 Bake in the oven for about 30–35 minutes, until the sausages are thoroughly cooked and the batter is risen and golden brown.

Bread and butter pudding (lower fat)

Although, as its name implies, this pudding is traditionally made with thickly buttered bread and is baked with full-cream milk, I decided to try lower-fat recipes using polyunsaturated margarine or very low fat spread and semi-skimmed milk. The lower-fat version is very good and can be eaten by people who are worried about saturated fat intake and might otherwise omit this delicious, simple pudding from their diet.

Serves 2

Oven temperature: 170°C, 325°F, gas mark 3

Cooking time: 30 minutes standing time plus 45 minutes to 1 hour in the oven

INGREDIENTS

3 slices white bread
1 oz (30 g) butter (or polyunsaturated margarine or very
   low fat spread)
1 oz (30 g) mixed dried fruit
1½ level tablespoons caster sugar
1 large egg
½ pint (285 ml) milk (full-cream or semi-skimmed)

METHOD

1 Cut the crusts off the bread, spread the slices with butter, margarine or low-fat spread, and cut into triangles or fingers.
2 Put half the bread, fat side up, into a greased heat-proof dish.
3 Sprinkle with the fruit and half the sugar.
4 Top with the rest of the bread and sprinkle with the rest of the sugar.
5 Beat the eggs and milk together and, using a nylon sieve, strain into the dish over the bread.
6 Leave to stand for about 30 minutes.
7 Bake for 45 minutes to 1 hour until the custard is set and the top crisp and golden.

Caramel custard

The addition of extra egg yolks to the whole eggs makes this a particularly creamy custard.

Serves 4–6

Oven temperature: 180°C, 350°F, gas mark 4

Cooking time: 45 minutes to 1 hour

You will need a soufflé dish about 7½ inches (19 cm) in diameter and a roasting tin for a bain-marie.

INGREDIENTS

For the caramel
3–4 oz (85–115 g) granulated or caster sugar

For the custard
2 whole eggs, size 2
2 egg yolks
2 tablespoons sugar
a few drops vanilla essence
1 pint (565 ml) milk

METHOD

To make the caramel
1 In a small saucepan just cover the sugar with cold water and bring to the boil, stirring to dissolve. Boil and bubble, without stirring, until a caramel colour. **Do not let the caramel get too dark or it will become bitter. As soon as it reaches a medium gold colour, remove from the heat and briefly**

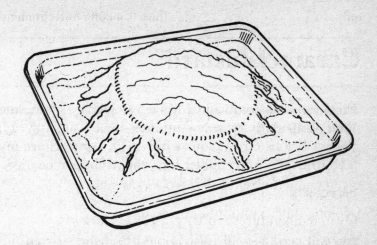

hold the saucepan under a dribble of cold water from the tap (take care, it may splutter).

2 Carefully pour the caramel into the warmed soufflé dish, turning swiftly to coat base and sides. Leave to cool.

To make the custard

3 In a bowl, beat the eggs, yolks, sugar and vanilla.

4 Bring the milk almost to the boil and, stirring, pour into the egg mixture.

5 Pour through a nylon sieve into the dish, breaking down any small bubbles.

6 Stand the dish in a roasting-tin containing warm water. Cover with a large piece of dampened grease-proof paper dipping into the water (see illustration).

7 Bake for 45 minutes to 1 hour, until the custard is set. (Test with a knife in the centre.)

8 Remove the soufflé dish from the tin and cool.

Fruit cobbler

Fresh apricots are inclined to be tasteless; by simmering them, unpeeled, for a few minutes in the sugar syrup, their delicious tart flavour is revealed. Apricots are my favourite for a fruit cobbler but other fruits can be used.

Serves 3–4

Oven temperature: 220°C, 425°F, gas mark 7

Cooking time: 10–15 minutes, after preliminary cooking

INGREDIENTS

1½ lb (680 g) apricots or plums
¼ cup sugar
1 oz (30 g) margarine
4 oz (115 g) self-raising flour
1 level tablespoon caster sugar
a scant 2 fl oz (50 ml) milk

METHOD

1 Halve and stone the apricots or plums. Bring the ¼ cup sugar to the boil with ¼ cup water, stirring; then add the chosen fruit and simmer long enough for it to become tender without losing its shape. Half fill an ovenproof dish with this fruit and some of the juice.

2 Rub the margarine into the flour until it has the texture of fine breadcrumbs. Stir in the level tablespoon sugar.

3 Stir in just sufficient milk to make a soft dough.

4 Knead on a lightly floured surface, pat or roll to ½ inch (1 cm) thick and cut into small scones with a 1½ inch (4 cm) fluted cutter.

5 Arrange these little scones around the edge of the dish, brushing each round with a little milk.

6 Bake for about 10–15 minutes until the scones are golden.

Variations

Fresh gooseberries may be somewhat sharp. I prefer to use *canned or bottled gooseberries*, with some of their syrup, for this recipe.

If using *fresh rhubarb and orange*, first cut the rhubarb into 1 inch (2.5 cm) lengths, then cover with boiling water. Leave for 5 minutes. Pour off the water and simmer the rhubarb with fresh orange, using a little of the grated rind, the cut-up orange and the juices running out from the cutting. When softened, sweeten to taste. Continue with steps 2–6.

Lemon meringue sponge

In my youth I gave my lemon meringue pie recipe to girlfriends who wanted to impress their beaux. Now that they all seem to be watching their waistlines, I have adapted it, using a fatless sponge instead of the rich pastry base.

For the sponge flan use half Gilly's sponge-cake recipe (page 254), or make two flans from the recipe and freeze one for later use. Or buy a ready-made sponge flan.

INGREDIENTS

For filling one flan
8 oz (225 g) caster sugar
grated rind and juice from 2 lemons
1 oz (30 g) butter
2 egg yolks
5–6 level tablespoons cornflour

Meringue topping
2 egg whites
2 oz (55 g) granulated sugar
2 oz (55 g) caster sugar
glacé cherries
angelica
extra caster sugar

METHOD

1 Make the sponge flan and turn out to cool. Or fight your way through the packaging of the ready-made flan!

2 Put the sugar, lemon rind and juice, butter and egg yolks in a saucepan, stir well to blend, then pour in ½ pint (285 ml) hot water and bring to the boil, stirring.

3 In a small bowl, blend the cornflour to a smooth cream with a little cold water.

4 Stir some of the hot lemon mixture into the cornflour, and then rapidly transfer it to the pan, stirring gently for 2–3 minutes. It needs to be thick enough not to seep into the sponge cake, so thicken with a little more cornflour in water if necessary.

5 When cool, spoon into the sponge flan.

6 To make the meringue topping: whisk the egg whites until they stand in stiff peaks, add the granulated sugar and whisk again. Fold in the caster sugar. Pile on top of the lemon, spreading to the edges to seal the filling completely.

7 Decorate with cherries and angelica, sprinkle with a little extra caster sugar and heat very gently under a cool grill until the meringue peaks go pale golden. Turn the flan if necessary for even colouring.

8 Serve cold.

Pancakes

You will need a 7 inch (18 cm) pan – preferably one kept specially for omelettes or pancakes.

Makes about 10 pancakes (but the first one often fails!)

INGREDIENTS

4 oz (115 g) plain flour, sifted
pinch salt
2 eggs
½ pint (285 ml) milk (full-cream or semi-skimmed)

For lemon pancakes, serve with caster sugar and lemon juice.

METHOD

1 **If using a food processor**, combine batter ingredients until smooth; pour into a jug. **If using a blender**, whiz all the batter ingredients except flour at maximum speed for a few seconds, add the flour in tablespoons and continue to blend for a further 30 seconds. Pour into a jug.

  If making by hand, sieve the flour and salt into a bowl, make a well in the centre, add the eggs and half the milk, gradually stir in the flour until smooth and beat with a wooden spoon until 'plopping' and bubbly. Gently stir in the rest of the milk. Pour into a jug.

2 Heat a little oil in the pan, barely covering the base (if it looks oily, wipe gently with kitchen paper so that only a thin film remains).

3 When very hot, pour in about 2 tablespoons of batter and swiftly tilt the pan around so that it is covered evenly.

4 Cook over high heat to brown underneath, about 1 minute.

5 Toss, or flip over with a palette knife. Cook the other side for about ½ minute. Turn on to greaseproof paper.

6 For lemon pancakes, roll them up after sprinkling liberally with caster sugar and lemon juice.

Home-made cooked pancakes can be kept for speedy entertaining: cool the cooked pancakes, interleaved with greaseproof paper or freezer interleaf film, before storing in fridge (5–6 days) or freezer (up to 6 months), sealed in foil or freezer bag. Frozen pancakes will thaw at room temperature in 10–15 minutes.

Thawed unwrapped pancakes can be reheated in foil in a moderate oven for 20–30 minutes, or fried in a lightly greased pan for about ½ minute each side. But I particularly like the recipe overleaf.

St Clement's pancakes

Serves 2

INGREDIENTS

1 ½ oz (45 g) butter
1 ½ oz (45 g) caster sugar
4 cooked pancakes, home-made or shop-bought
grated rind and juice of 1 orange
grated rind and juice of ½ lemon
a dash of Grand Marnier or Cointreau (optional)

METHOD

1 Heat the butter gently in a frying-pan; stir in the sugar.
2 Fold the cooked pancakes in quarters, place in the pan and fry over low heat for about a minute.
3 Add the fruit juice and rind (and liqueur), and bring to the boil. Serve piping hot.

Plum and apple crumble

Serves 2–3

Oven temperature: 190°C, 375°F, gas mark 5

Cooking time: about 50 minutes

INGREDIENTS

6–8 oz (170–225 g) plums
6–8 oz (170–225 g) cooking apples
1 oz (30 g) granulated sugar
scant 1 ½ oz (35 g) butter or margarine
1 ½ oz (45 g) flour (wholemeal, white or a mixture of both)
1 ½ oz (45 g) porridge oats
½ teaspoon cinnamon
1 oz (30 g) demerara sugar

METHOD

1 Halve and stone the plums. Peel, core and slice the apples. Put the fruit with the granulated sugar in an ovenproof dish.
2 Rub the butter or margarine into the mixed flour, porridge oats and cinnamon. Stir in the demerara sugar.
3 Sprinkle this crumble over the fruit.
4 Bake for about 50 minutes, until the fruit is soft and juicy and the topping crunchy.

Rice pudding (made with semi-skimmed milk)

For those who are cutting down on their intake of saturated fats, the following recipe substitutes semi-skimmed milk for full-cream milk. With this lower-fat milk, a higher proportion of rice has to be used.

Serves 2–3 (quantities can be halved in a smaller dish for 1 large or 2 small portions)

Oven temperature: 150°C, 300°F, gas mark 2

Cooking time: 2–2½ hours, plus 30 minutes preliminary cooking (1 hour by speedier method, plus 15 minutes preliminary cooking)

INGREDIENTS

2 oz (55 g) pudding rice
1 pint (565 ml) semi-skimmed milk
1 oz (30 g) caster sugar
1 strip lemon rind
grated nutmeg

METHOD

1 Wash the rice through a sieve. Put into a 1½ pint (0.9 litre) greased ovenproof dish and stir in the milk. Leave to soak for 30 minutes.

2 Meanwhile, pre-heat the oven to 150°C, 300°F, gas mark 2.

3 Add the sugar and lemon rind to the rice, stir well and sprinkle the top with nutmeg.

4 Place in the centre of the preheated oven and bake for 2–2½ hours. Stir in the skin two or three times during the first hour.

Speedier method

If you do not object to washing up an extra saucepan, you can easily halve the cooking time by this alternative method.

1 Set the oven to 150°C, 300°F, gas mark 2. Lightly grease a 1½ pint (0.9 litre) ovenproof dish.

2 Wash the rice through a sieve. Put into a small saucepan with the milk, sugar and lemon rind, and simmer very gently in the covered pan, with occasional stirring, for 15 minutes.

3 Transfer to the greased oven dish. Stir, sprinkle with a little grated nutmeg and bake, stirring once or twice more, until the rice is tender and the milk absorbed (about 1 hour).

Spotted Dick

An alternative name for a large Spotted Dick is Spotted Dog, so in our family these small individual puddings are known affectionately as Spotted Puppies. But they can be 'vegetable' rather than 'animal' because they can be made with shredded vegetable suet in preference to the traditional beef suet.

Serves 3

To serve three individual Spotted Puppies, you will need three ¼ pint (140 ml) pudding basins.

INGREDIENTS

1 ½ oz (45 g) vegetable suet
1 ½ oz (45 g) fresh breadcrumbs
1 ½ oz (45 g) self-raising flour
pinch of salt
1 oz (30 g) caster sugar
3 oz (85 g) currants
about 3–4 tablespoons milk

Serve with butter and brown sugar *or* sweet white sauce flavoured with rum *or* Vanilla Sauce (see page 206) *or* pouring custard.

METHOD

1 Lightly grease the pudding basins.
2 Mix all the ingredients with sufficient milk to make a
   soft dropping consistency.*
3 Divide the mixture between the basins. Cover with
   strong foil, pleated and greased in the centre to allow
   for expansion during cooking (see illustration).

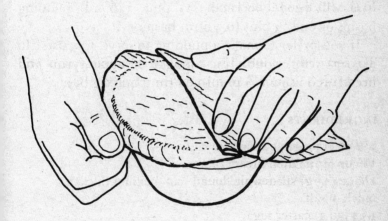

4 Steam over rapidly boiling water for 1 hour (keep the
   boiling water topped up if there is much evaporation).
5 Serve traditionally with butter and brown sugar or
   with your chosen pouring sauce.

* Note: for a lighter texture, mix at slow speed with an electric
beater.

Summer puddings

There are many recipes for summer puddings, using a variety of summer fruits, but my family's favourite is sharp and tangy, made only with blackcurrants.

Serves 2

You will need two small (¼ pint, 140 ml) pudding basins or one ½ pint (0.3 litre) basin.

   If you prefer to make a pudding to serve 4–6, use 1 lb (450 g) fruit, double the amount of sugar syrup and bread, and use a 1½ pint (0.9 litre) pudding basin.

INGREDIENTS

6–8 oz (170–225 g) blackcurrants
½ cup granulated sugar
about 4 large slices white bread (cut medium thick)*

METHOD

1 Use a fork to help remove the blackcurrants from their stalks. Wash in a sieve.
2 Bring ¼ cup water to the boil with the sugar, add the fruit and gently simmer until the juices run and the currants retain their shape but are tender.
3 Remove the crusts from the bread and use it to line the bottom and sides of the basin.

---

* This needs to be slightly stale. My daughter's tip: freeze the sliced loaf, return some separated slices to room temperature and leave for a few hours.

4 Pour in half the blackcurrants and juice and cover
   with another slice of bread (half a slice may be
   sufficient for small puddings). Pour in the remainder
   of the fruit and sufficient juice to moisten very well.
5 Score the bread around the rim of the basin and fold
   over to cover the pudding. Finish with a final half or
   full slice of bread on top.
6 Fit a saucer on top, weighted down (e.g. with a
   weight from the kitchen scales). Leave to cool.
7 When cold, either turn out or serve direct from the
   basin.

These puddings freeze well. Cover them first; defrost
at room temperature.

Semolina pudding (made with semi-skimmed milk)

This method calls for dedicated stirring, but it gives a smooth, creamy pudding. To cut down on fat in this recipe, I used semi-skimmed milk: note that it needs 5 tablespoons of semolina to thicken, instead of the usual 4 tablespoons recommended with full-cream milk.

Serves 2–3

INGREDIENTS

1 pint (565 ml) semi-skimmed milk
small knob of margarine
5 level tablespoons semolina
6 level tablespoons sugar

Serve with a spoonful of jam (our family favourite is blackcurrant jam with port).

METHOD

1 Heat the milk and margarine and sprinkle the semolina on top.
2 Bring to simmering point, stirring, and simmer very gently with constant stirring for at least 15 minutes, until it thickens.
3 Stir in the sugar and serve immediately in warmed bowls, accompanied by a pot of jam.

Chapter Four
Cooking for Children

FAMILY MEALS WITH CHILDREN IN MIND

Store-cupboard tomato soup
Carrot and peanut-butter soup
Cheese puffs
Fishcakes
Tuna-fish pie
Tuna-filled pitta
Crispy chicken breasts
Chicken cooked in ginger ale
Beefburgers
Beany cottage pie
Lamb layer
Fruit and custard puddings
Pink apple

CHILDREN'S PARTIES

Cheese pastry shapes
Sandwiches
  'my house'
  toys' tea-party

ribbon
rolled frankfurter
Raw vegetables with dips
Hard-boiled mice
Cucumber monsters
Carrot and cucumber sticks
Shark-infested jelly
Tilted jelly
Striped meringues
Bite-sized buns
Baked Alaska
Sue's home-made lemonade/ lemonade ice lollies

FOR YOUNG COOKS

Children who are visiting grandparents, godparents, 'courtesy aunts' and other retired relatives or family friends might enjoy learning cookery techniques and helping to prepare any of the recipes in this book. The following extra recipes are chosen to be more like play than work. Cooking should be fun.

Easy pizzas
Bread bunnies
Decorated eggs
    stuffed eggs
    egg sandwiches
    golden eggs
Segmenting an orange
Flapjacks
Rock buns

Fancy shaped biscuits
   Playdoh-cutter biscuits
   traffic-light biscuits
Marion's painted biscuits
Chocolate krackolates (unbaked)
Fairy cakes
Melting moments
Chocolate-dipped fruit
Witches' cake
Marshmallow sticks

The ideas for this chapter (favourites with my two daughters and their friends) were first discussed with a former colleague, Mrs Sue Thomas, State Registered Dietitian. She added some of her own recipes – tempting and nutritious – which she cooks for her young family. The next stage was a taste panel with her neighbours and their children. Their comments were sometimes critical, frequently appreciative and always honest! They are included with my grateful thanks.

Store-cupboard tomato soup

Serves 2–3 (for 1 serving halve the quantities and use a small (230 g) can of tomatoes)

INGREDIENTS

1 small onion, peeled and sliced
½ clove garlic, finely chopped (optional)
¼–½ teaspoon mixed dried herbs
1 tablespoon oil
1 medium (14 oz, 400 g) can peeled tomatoes
salt, pepper and a large pinch of sugar
about 1 teacup milk

METHOD

1 In a covered pan, gently cook the onion, garlic and herbs in the oil until softened but not brown.
2 Add the tomatoes with their juice, chopping them roughly before bringing to the boil.
3 Purée* or sieve.
4 Return to the pan, season with the salt, pepper and sugar, and dilute to taste with milk, heating to just below boiling point.

* For speed use an electric blender; for those who dislike all pips, strain the resultant purée through a nylon sieve before returning it to the pan.

Carrot/peanut-butter soup

This recipe was first presented by the Dairy Produce Advisory Service of the Milk Marketing Board as part of a review outlining the nutritional requirements of children aged between one and five. The recipes translated principles into practice. Carrot and Peanut Soup was devised to meet the needs of a lively 2½-year-old who had just learnt to say NO! She was eating family food but was very fussy.

Serves 2 adults and 1 child

INGREDIENTS

½ medium onion, peeled and chopped or sliced
12 oz (340 g) carrots, peeled and chopped or sliced
½ pint (285 ml) stock
1 tablespoon *smooth* peanut butter
½ pint (285 ml) fresh milk
for topping: natural yogurt and parsley

METHOD

1 Place the vegetables in a pan with the stock and peanut butter. Bring to the boil and simmer for approximately 15 minutes, until softened.
2 Liquidize until smooth. Pour back into the pan, stir in the milk and reheat without boiling.
3 It can be served topped with a swirl of yogurt and sprinkled with snipped parsley.

Cheese puffs

A savoury change from sweet biscuits. They keep well in an airtight container.

Makes 25–30 small triangles (allow 2 or more per serving)

Oven temperature: 200° C, 400° F, gas mark 6

Cooking time: about 15 minutes

INGREDIENTS

8 oz (225 g) ready-made puff pastry (defrosted if frozen)
3 oz (85 g) grated cheese

METHOD

1 Roll out the pastry fairly thinly. Spread half of it with one third of the grated cheese. Fold over and roll out again.
2 Spread half the pastry with half the remaining grated cheese. Fold over and roll out.
3 Spread half the pastry with the last of the grated cheese, fold and roll out. Then fold and roll once again to ensure that the cheese is well incorporated into the pastry.
4 Cut into triangles and bake on a greased baking sheet for about 15 minutes until puffed and golden brown.

Fishcakes

Makes 6

INGREDIENTS

10 oz (285 g) cooked and flaked white fish, e.g. cod
10 oz (285 g) boiled potato, mashed with butter
2 oz (55 g) cooked peas
2 oz (55 g) cooked, finely diced carrot
if necessary, beaten egg to bind
packet dry stuffing mixture
oil and margarine

Serve with salad or cooked green vegetables.

METHOD

1 Combine the fish, potato, peas and carrots together in a bowl. If the mixture seems too dry, add a little beaten egg.
2 Divide and shape into 6 fishcakes. Coat with a thin layer of stuffing mixture.
3 Shallow-fry for 10 minutes, turning during cooking.

Suggestion: prepare a batch of fishcakes and freeze extra ones for quick after-school teas.

Tuna-fish pie

Serves 2 adults and 1 child

Oven temperature: 220°C, 425°F, gas mark 7

Cooking time: about 25 minutes

INGREDIENTS

1 ½ lb (675 g) creamy mashed potato
3 hard-boiled eggs, sliced (1 per person)
7 oz (200 g) can tuna in oil*
3 firm tomatoes, skinned and thinly sliced

METHOD

1 Line the bottom of a pie dish with a thick layer of just over half the mashed potatoes. Cover with the sliced hard-boiled eggs.
2 Add the flaked tuna, well drained of its oil.
3 Cover with the peeled sliced tomatoes.
4 Top with a final layer of mashed potatoes.
5 Bake in the oven until nicely browned on top.

Serve with a favourite sauce and vegetables.

Extra comments from neighbour who was chief taster with daughter Jessica: tuna in oil, once drained, did not make the dish too greasy. The quantity was just right and it appealed to the adults as well as to Jessica.

* Nutrition note: tuna in oil is to be preferred to tuna in brine because nutritionists tend to discourage salt for children.

Tuna-filled pitta

Serves 2 adults and 1–2 children (or 3 teenagers – younger children might find it too difficult to handle)

INGREDIENTS

7 oz (200 g) can tuna fish in oil, drained
3 oz (85 g) Red Leicester cheese, grated
1 teaspoon lemon juice
5 fl oz (140 ml) natural yogurt
2 level tablespoons parsley, chopped
pepper
pitta bread (white or brown)
lettuce
tomato and cucumber slices

METHOD

1 Mash the tuna in a bowl with the cheese, lemon juice, yogurt and parsley. Season to taste with pepper.
2 Make a slit along the long edge of the pitta bread to form a pocket. Place some lettuce inside and spread on a portion of the fish mixture.
3 Arrange tomato and cucumber slices on top of the fish.

Crispy chicken breasts

Serves 2–3, or 4–6 small portions

Oven temperature: 180°C, 350°F, gas mark 4

Cooking time: 30 minutes

INGREDIENTS

2–3 boned, skinned chicken breast fillets
1 small bag (30 g) plain potato crisps
about 1 oz (30 g) grated Cheddar cheese
1 egg, beaten

METHOD

1 Wash and dry the chicken.
2 Crush the potato crisps and mix on a plate with the grated cheese.
3 Dip the chicken into the beaten egg and then into the crisp and cheese mixture.
4 Place on a greased baking dish and bake uncovered for approximately 30 minutes, to cook the chicken and crisp the coating.

Verdict: lovely recipe, ideal for children. When catering for 3–6 year olds, one chicken breast, preferably split before cooking, served two children adequately.

Chicken cooked in ginger ale

I like to challenge teenage visitors to guess what liquid has made the gravy!

Serves 3

Cooking time: 45 minutes, after preliminary frying

INGREDIENTS

3 chicken portions
small knob butter or margarine
1 onion, sliced
3 oz (85 g) mushrooms, sliced
1 chicken stock cube
1 small can (330 ml) dry ginger ale
3 tablespoons rice
frozen sweetcorn, peas and carrots, or other mixed
    vegetables

METHOD

1 Lightly brown the chicken pieces in a little butter or margarine. During cooking, add the onion and mushrooms to soften.
2 Add the chicken stock cube, pour the ginger ale over gradually (it will fizz at first), heat and stir to dissolve the cube. Simmer for 25 minutes with the lid on the pan.
3 Stir in the raw rice, and continue to simmer for 15 minutes.
4 Add the frozen vegetables. Bring back to the boil and simmer for another 5 minutes, or according to packet instructions. Taste for flavour and serve hot.

Beefburgers

Home-made beefburgers seem to be liked by children of all ages, but onion is seldom a popular ingredient with the very young: 1–2 shallots are usually sufficient in a 1 lb (450 g) mixture.

Beefburgers may be served as a main meal with mashed potato and vegetables, as a high tea with oven chips and baked beans, or in wholemeal pitta-bread envelopes with raw slices of cucumber and grated carrot.

Makes 8–10 beefburgers for small appetites; older children may manage 2 or more at a sitting

INGREDIENTS

1 lb (450 g) minced beef
1–2 shallots, or ½ small onion, very finely chopped
2 oz (55 g) wholemeal breadcrumbs*
a dash of Worcestershire sauce
2–3 tablespoons milk to bind
salt and pepper
butter or corn oil for frying

* Or soak 2 oz (55 g) bread in a little water, squeeze out and mash.

METHOD

1 Mix all the beefburger ingredients together with a fork.

2 Using floured hands, divide the mixture into 8–10 thick flat rounds. Cook or freeze (see next step).

3 *To cook*: heat butter or oil in a shallow pan and fry in the hot fat for 5–6 minutes on each side; alternatively, cook under a hot grill for 5–6 minutes on each side.

To freeze: place the raw beefburgers, slightly apart, on foil-lined baking sheets, and freeze uncovered until hard. When frozen, wrap separately in film or interleaf wrap, then pack together in a freezer bag. Unpack, then fry or grill from frozen, allowing 8 minutes on each side to cook thoroughly.

Comments from a godmother: for children addicted to the takeaway burger bar, it is highly advisable to serve home-made beefburgers in an appropriate bap or bun, with their favourite garnishes such as shredded lettuce, slices of cheese or tomato, dill pickles, and the age-old favourite, tomato ketchup.

Beany cottage pie

The addition of baked beans to this traditional dish makes it more interesting for many children.

Serves 2–3

Oven temperature: 190°C, 375°F, gas mark 5

Cooking time: 20–30 minutes, after preliminary frying

INGREDIENTS

8 oz. (225 g) minced beef
2 shallots or ½ small onion, finely chopped
1 teaspoon Bovril dissolved in ¼ pint (140 ml) boiling water
pinch mixed herbs
2 teaspoons tomato ketchup
dash Worcestershire sauce
small can (5 oz, 140 g) baked beans
pepper
1 lb (450 g) creamy mashed potato

METHOD

1 Brown the mince in a frying-pan over a fast heat.
2 Reduce the heat and add the onion; continue to fry for a further 10 minutes.
3 Pour the Bovril over the meat and add the herbs, ketchup, Worcestershire sauce, baked beans and pepper.
4 Place the meat mixture into the base of a medium-sized casserole, or into individual ramekin dishes

(4 inches, 10 cm in diameter) for special appeal to children.

5 Top with mashed potato and fork evenly over the meat mixture.

6 Bake uncovered in a fairly hot oven for 20–30 minutes.

Variations

I was given this tip from a grandmother whose small grandchild adores Beany Cottage Pie, but refuses green vegetables if they are served separately with it: place a layer of lightly cooked sliced cabbage on top of the meat mixture before you top it with the mashed potato.

Another well-received variation: to add 'crunch appeal' crush some potato crisps and sprinkle them on top of the mashed potato before baking.

Lamb layer

A tasty way of extending a small amount of meat left over from the Sunday roast.

Serves 2–3

Oven temperature: 190°C, 375°F, gas mark 5 for 30 minutes, then raise to 200°C, 400°F, gas mark 6 for 30 minutes

Total cooking time: 1 hour

INGREDIENTS

1 medium onion, diced
1 oz (30 g) butter
8 oz (225 g) cooked lamb, finely diced
pinch of mixed herbs
2 level tablespoons tomato purée
1 teaspoon Worcestershire sauce
salt and pepper
1 lb (450 g) potatoes, boiled and sliced
8 oz (225 g) can chopped tomatoes
5 fl oz (140 ml) natural yogurt
1 egg, beaten

METHOD

1 Cook the onion gently in the butter. Add the meat, herbs, tomato purée and Worcestershire sauce. Season to taste.
2 In a 2 pint (1.1 litre) ovenproof casserole, arrange a layer of half the potatoes, then the meat mixture, followed by the tomatoes with their juice, and finish

with a layer of potatoes. Cover and bake in the oven at 190°C, 375°F, gas mark 5 for 30 minutes.

3 Blend the yogurt into the egg. Season to taste and spoon over the potatoes. Return to the oven to cook, uncovered, at 200°C, 400°F, gas mark 6 for a further 30 minutes.

Alternatively, serve thin slices of cold meat with plenty of vegetables.

Choose from:
   Carrot and Courgette Fritters (page 15)
   Bubble and Squeak (page 74)
   Peas in the French Fashion (page 182)
   Ratatouille Bake (page 184)
   Mixed Steamed Vegetables with Herb Butter (page 286)
   Honeyed Potatoes (page 23)
   Rice and Potatoes (page 76)
   Sliced Roast Potatoes (page 288).

Fruit and custard puddings

Serves 4

Oven temperature: 170° C, 325° F, gas mark 3

Cooking time: 45–50 minutes

You will need 4 individual ramekin dishes.

INGREDIENTS

For the custards
3 eggs, size 2
1–2 tablespoons caster sugar
12 fl oz (340 ml) milk (whole or semi-skimmed)*
a few drops vanilla essence

For the topping
small knob butter
1 ½ teaspoons demerara sugar
1 oz (30 g) desiccated coconut
raspberries or other soft fruit

Alternative topping
1–2 bananas
fromage frais, yogurt or whipped cream

METHOD

1 Whisk eggs and sugar together and whisk in the milk
  and vanilla.
2 Strain into a jug through a sieve.

* Nutrition note: under-fives need whole milk; use either whole or
semi-skimmed milk for over-fives.

3 Pour into ramekin dishes and place in a roasting-tin half full of water.

4 Bake in the oven until set, approximately 45 minutes. Remove from the heat and leave to cool. Turn out into individual bowls for serving.

To make the topping

Melt the butter, add the sugar and coconut, and fry gently until the coconut has browned, stirring all the time. It will brown fairly rapidly. Pile the raspberries on top of the cooled custards and spoon the coconut over.

Alternative simple topping

For those who do not like coconut or the pips in raspberries, substitute a simple topping of mashed or sliced banana with fromage frais, yogurt or whipped cream, sweetened if necessary.

Pink apple

Serves 2 – serve hot or cold

INGREDIENTS

2 medium to large cooking apples
1 large tablespoon redcurrant jelly
sugar to taste

METHOD

1 Core and peel the apples and cut into quarters.
2 Stew in a little water in a covered pan until fluffy.*
3 With a whisk, incorporate the redcurrant jelly and
  sugar to taste.

* Note: the amount of water will depend on the variety of apple: it
needs to be just sufficient to be absorbed by the apples while they
are cooking, leaving them juicy but not runny. Sugar should not
be added during the cooking because it prevents the apples from
breaking down.

Cheese pastry shapes

These make a tasty alternative to crisps and other packet snacks.

Oven temperature: 200°C, 400°F, gas mark 6

Cooking time: approximately 10 minutes

INGREDIENTS

4 oz (115 g) plain flour
pinch of salt
2 oz (55 g) butter or block margarine, cut in pieces
1½ oz (45 g) grated Cheddar cheese
beaten egg to bind and glaze

METHOD

1 Sift the flour and salt into a mixing bowl and rub in the fat until the mixture resembles breadcrumbs.
2 With a fork, stir in the grated cheese.
3 Stir in a little beaten egg, until the mixture binds to a firm dough.
4 Roll out the dough on a floured surface to ⅓ inch (1 cm) thickness.
5 Using small cocktail cutters (e.g. stars, moons, heart shapes), cut out tiny cheese pastry shapes. Lightly brush each shape with beaten egg. Place on a greased baking tray and bake for 10 minutes or until lightly brown.

Sandwiches

While young children are eating 'My House' sandwiches, or tiny tea-party sandwiches, older children can
be enjoying ribbon sandwiches or rolled frankfurters.
Their parents can be served with open sandwiches or
small bridge rolls.

'My house' sandwich

Small children with reluctant appetites may be tempted
by 'My House'. (Even children who live under flat
roofs without open fires seem to draw houses with
pitched roofs and chimneys, so that is the pattern I
use!)

Butter a slice of bread and cut off the crusts. Shape
the roof and chimney (see illustration). With a knife,
daub in the front door and windows with Marmite and
the roof and chimney with smooth peanut butter. Other
spreads can be used if preferred, for example sweet
chocolate spread or savoury sandwich spread (excellent
for the roof tiles).

Toys' tea-party sandwiches

Cut up sandwiches into tiny bites, not more than
¾ inch (2 cm) square.

Use thin-cut bread spread sparingly with margarine
or softened butter. Add a thin spread for ease of handling, for example Marmite, cream cheese, smooth

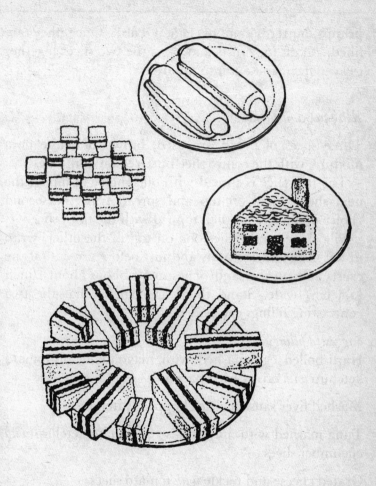

peanut butter,* jam or lemon curd. Once they are
filled, cut off the crusts and press the two slices together
to keep firm, and cut into squares.

Ribbon sandwiches

Three slices of bread are used, brown or white or a
mixture, with the centre slice buttered on both sides.

The first slice is spread with one choice of filling, the
next slice is laid on top and spread with the second
choice of filling, and then topped with the third slice.

Pile these sandwiches one on top of the other, wrap
in foil in the refrigerator, and just before use cut off the
crusts and cut the sandwiches into ribbons about 1 inch
(2.5 cm) wide. Stand them on edge so that the two
contrasting fillings can be seen.

Suggested fillings

Hard-boiled egg mashed with mayonnaise or tomato
ketchup *with* crispy fried bacon

Mashed liver sausage *with* chopped watercress

Tuna mashed with mayonnaise or tomato ketchup *with*
cucumber slices

Grated cheese and pickle *with* tomato slices

Mashed or sliced banana *with* cream cheese mixed with
finely chopped dates or raisins.

* For young children it is advisable to avoid the nuts in chunky
peanut butter.

Rolled frankfurter sandwiches

Use fresh, thinly sliced bread from a large loaf. Roll out gently with a rolling-pin to make it more pliable. Butter right to the edge, and then cut off the crusts. Spread with a little tomato ketchup and carefully roll up round the cooked frankfurters, pressing down the long buttered end to prevent it from unrolling. Wrap in foil or waxed paper and refrigerate. They can be cut in half for daintier appetites.

Small bridge rolls and open sandwiches

See pages 227–9

Raw vegetables with dips

Serving a selection of cut-up raw vegetables is also a cunning way of tempting children to nibble a few vegetables while you serve drinks before a family lunch party – they may happily accept the vegetables that might otherwise be rejected during the main meal!

For adults and children, the raw vegetables can be served with a dip made of 3 tablespoons thick shop-bought mayonnaise, 3 tablespoons fromage frais, about 2 tablespoons tomato ketchup, 2 teaspoons tomato purée and a dash of Worcestershire sauce.

Hard-boiled mice

INGREDIENTS

eggs (as many as you wish)
raw carrot
chives
flaked almonds (optional)
dried currants
ingredients for a cheese salad, e.g. lettuce or other salad
    leaves, grated carrots, cooked peas, cubed or grated
    cheese, salad dressing

METHOD

1 Hard-boil the eggs, cool them under running water
   and peel them carefully.
2 Slice the eggs in half lengthwise. Lay them in the
   centre of the serving plate.

3 Prepare the mice (see illustration).

To make the ears, *either* insert a flaked almond for each ear just above the narrow end, *or* cut two raw carrot slices and then cut a point in each slice to stick in the egg.

Stick two currants into each mouse for eyes.

For whiskers, cut six short lengths of chive and push in with the help of a cocktail stick.

Cut one long chive for the tail.

4 Serve the mice surrounded by a cheese salad.

Cucumber monsters

While you are preparing the lunch or tea, provide the older children with a fresh cucumber, misshapen if possible. This they can turn into a 'monster' by spearing radishes, cubes of cheese, chunks of carrot and other vegetables or fruits on to short cocktail sticks and inserting them into the cucumber for eyes, nose, ears, legs, scales, tail or any other appendages belonging to a monster.

Carrot and cucumber sticks

Children's parties seldom contain any fresh vegetables. Chunky sticks of cucumber and 2 inch (5 cm) long matchsticks of raw carrots always seem to be a popular teatime item.

Shark-infested jelly

Look around the sweetshops and supermarkets for the new shapes in jelly sweets. I have found, for instance, sharks and crocs and monsters to add to the usual range of jelly babies.

I had no compunction in 'drowning' sharks and jelly monsters (for the sharks obviously it had to be in a sea-green jelly and for the monsters I used a yellow or orange jelly for an eerie effect). I drew the line at immersing jelly babies until my literary-minded son-in-law mentioned *The Water-Babies* . . . !

You will need 1 large glass bowl or small individual glasses (preferably a toughened glass such as Pyrex).

INGREDIENTS

2 or 3 packets of jelly (depending on size of party)
packets of sharks and crocs or other shapes

METHOD

1 Melt the jelly in boiling water as instructed on the packet before making up to the required amount with cold water (for a 1 pint jelly make up to only ¾ pint, 425 ml to ensure a good set).
2 When on the point of setting, add the sharks and crocs. If you prefer the appearance of a turbulent sea, stir in the sharks and crocs and a little later swirl them around with a fork.

If using individual glasses, immerse one shark or croc for each child.

Quick tip: to make a jelly set quickly, after dissolving the cubes in boiling water, make up to the required mark with ice cubes instead of cold water. Stir until the ice cubes have dissolved.

Fresh orange jelly

Pour freshly squeezed orange juice into ice-cube trays and freeze until needed.

For a set-while-you-watch jelly, place a packet of orange jelly in a measuring jug. Pour on boiling water up to the ½ pint mark and stir until dissolved. Then make up to just over ¾ pint with the iced orange juice cubes, stirring rapidly to dissolve. (For very young children you may wish to reduce the strong orange flavour by cooling with some orange ice cubes and some plain ice cubes.)

As an alternative to the jelly sweets, you can 'drown' some fruit in the jelly as it is on the point of setting. Suggestions: drained canned mandarin oranges, sliced banana, chopped peeled dessert apple.

Tilted jelly

You will need a large clear glass serving bowl.

INGREDIENTS

3 jellies of contrasting colours (e.g. red, yellow, green)*
optional: hundreds and thousands, or fruits for an
    accompanying fresh fruit salad

METHOD

1 Make up the first jelly as directed on the packet, using the smaller recommended amount of water so that it will set firmly.
2 Pour into the clear glass bowl and put it in a cool place or refrigerator to set, **with the bowl tilted at an angle**, propping it up firmly.
3 Make up the second jelly. Allow it to cool, but before it sets, tilt the bowl in the opposite direction, pour in the second jelly at the new angle and leave to set.
4 Make up the third jelly in the same way and when it has cooled but not yet set, stand the bowl upright and pour in the jelly to set.
5 If you want to be a 'supergran' sprinkle the set jelly with hundreds and thousands.

Turn the glass bowl round slowly so that the children can see the changing kaleidoscope.

* Notes: if you want to make a smaller jelly use half of each packet. You may want to alter the jelly colours to match the fruits in season.

Striped meringues

Makes approximately 25 small meringues

Oven temperature: 110–120°C, 225–250°F, gas mark
¼–½ (turn to the lower temperature if the meringues
begin to brown too quickly)

Cooking time: about 1¼ hours

You will need non-stick baking paper.

INGREDIENTS

3 egg whites
3 oz (85 g) granulated sugar
3 oz (85 g) caster sugar
pink food colouring*
blue food colouring*
a little extra sugar

METHOD

1 Line baking sheets with non-stick baking paper.
2 Whisk the egg whites very stiffly.
3 Add the granulated sugar and whisk briefly until the
   mixture regains its stiffness.
4 Divide the mixture between two bowls.
    In each bowl: lightly fold in half the caster sugar;
   add a few drops of food colouring (pink in one bowl

* Any combination of colours can be used for striped meringues,
although I know that some parents would prefer to avoid even
these few drops of food colouring: they could just make the white
meringue shapes without stripes.

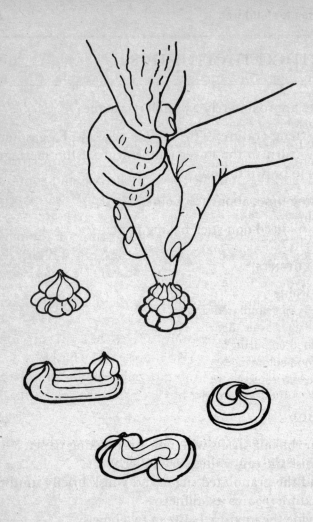

and blue in the other). Mix swiftly and lightly so that the colour is not amalgamated but shows in dark and light stripes.

For striped meringues

5 Pipe the blue mixture in a forcing bag* in a selection of patterns (see illustration). Before all the mixture is used, add the pink meringue to the bag and continue to pipe so that some have blue stripes, some are mixtures of blue and pink, and some have pink stripes.

   For further variety you can pipe some of the pink-striped mixture on top of the already piped blue.

For 'Baby in the Bath' meringues

Fill *two* forcing bags,* one with the blue mixture and one with the pink.

6 Pipe strips approximately 2½ inches (6 cm) long from each forcing bag – to represent the baths.

7 Put a pink blob for the girl baby in the blue bath, and a blue blob for the boy baby in the pink bath.

Both recipes

3 Before baking, sprinkle the meringues lightly with caster sugar; this helps to crisp them.

* To keep both hands free to fill the forcing bag, balance the bag like a bin-liner in a tall jug.

Bite-sized buns

Most small children love tiny iced buns made in petits fours cases, decorated with glacé icing (made from icing sugar and water) and with a single Smartie or jelly sweet on top. These are ideal for handing round the whole class on your grandchild's birthday. Use the easy all-in-one recipe given below.

Makes approximately 40–44 tiny buns

Oven temperature: 170°C, 325°F, gas mark 3

Cooking time: about 10–15 minutes

You will need paper petits fours cases and a baking sheet.

INGREDIENTS

4 oz (115 g) self-raising flour
½ teaspoon baking powder
4 oz (115 g) soft margarine
4 oz (115 g) caster sugar
2 eggs (size 3)

Icing
2–3 oz (55–85 g) icing sugar
approximately 1 tablespoon warm water or orange juice
jelly sweets or Smarties

METHOD

1 Preheat the oven.
2 Sift flour and baking powder into a mixing bowl.
3 Beat the flour with the soft margarine, sugar and eggs until smooth and well mixed.
4 Using two teaspoons, two thirds fill the paper cases, standing each on the baking sheet.
5 Bake for about 10–15 minutes, until risen and golden. Put aside to cool.
6 For the icing: gradually add the water or juice to the sifted icing sugar until thick enough to coat the back of a spoon.
7 Arrange the buns on a flat surface and drizzle icing on the top of each. Decorate with a sweet.

Baked Alaska

This is an exciting surprise cake: meringue hiding the cold ice-cream.

Serves 6–8

Oven temperature: 230°C, 450°F, gas mark 8

Cooking time: 3–5 minutes, just to brown the meringue

INGREDIENTS

7 inch (18 cm) sponge flan case (ready bought or home made, see page 254)
11 oz (310 g) can mandarin segments
a block or large tub (500 ml) vanilla ice-cream
4 egg whites/6 oz (170 g) caster sugar *or* 1 carton (320 g) meringue mix*

METHOD

1 Preheat the oven.
2 Place the sponge flan on a flat ovenproof dish, standing it on a baking tray. Sprinkle with enough juice from the can to moisten the sponge without making it soggy.
3 Cover completely with circles of the drained fruit.

* More than sufficient for a 7 inch flan. Because of the short cooking time, I recommend the use of a meringue mix containing pasteurized egg whites if there is considered to be any risk of salmonella for young children.

4 *Either* whisk the egg whites stiffly, then whisk in half
the sugar and fold in the rest of the sugar *or* whisk the
meringue mix, following the instructions on the
carton (this could take 10–12 minutes using an electric whisk).

5 With an ice-cream scoop pile up the ice-cream in
layers in the centre of the sponge, leaving the rim
clear.(Quick tip: ice-cream from a large round carton
approximately 5 inches in diameter can be inverted
whole on the flan.)

6 Swiftly pile the meringue mixture over the fruit, ice-
cream and flan so that they are *completely* masked and
the meringue touches down on the flan rim.

7 Immediately bake in the oven for about 3 minutes,
just until the meringue begins to brown on the outside
without melting the ice-cream. Serve at once.

Sue's home-made lemonade/ lemonade ice lollies

This recipe makes about 1 pint (0.6 litre) cordial, which is then diluted. If available, choose unwaxed fruit.

INGREDIENTS

2 lemons (see stage 4)
1 large orange
4 oz (115 g) granulated or caster sugar
½ level teaspoon citric-acid powder

METHOD

1 Scrub the fruit thoroughly in cold water.
2 Using a potato peeler, finely peel the lemons and orange, taking care not to remove the pith as well.
3 Place the peel and sugar in a saucepan with ¾ pint (425 ml) water. Bring to the boil, remove from the heat, cover and leave to infuse for 45 minutes.
4 Meanwhile squeeze a scant 3 tablespoons of lemon juice and add all the juice from the orange.
5 Strain the infusion through a sieve to remove the peel. Add the juices and citric-acid powder. Stir well.
6 Dilute and taste and serve with ice.

Lemonade ice lollies

The above cordial, diluted with equal parts water, poured into lolly moulds and frozen makes delicious lemonade ice lollies.

Easy pizzas

INGREDIENTS

pitta bread (brown or white)
tomato purée
a sprinkle of oregano
peeled and finely sliced tomatoes
canned sweetcorn
sliced mushrooms*
sliced salami, ham or smoked bacon
olives*
grated cheese

METHOD

1 Spread the pitta bread with a thin smear of tomato purée, sprinkle lightly with oregano and let the children add their favourite extras such as those itemized in the ingredients above.
2 Grill until bubbling hot.

* For the more adventurous.

Bread bunnies

Left-over bunnies can be frozen for serving another day. Once thawed, refresh in a moderate oven for 10 minutes.

Makes 8

Oven temperature: 230°C, 450°F, gas mark 8

Cooking time: 35 minutes to prove followed by 15 minutes baking.

You will need two lightly oiled baking sheets.

INGREDIENTS

280 g packet white or brown bread mix

Serve with butter and salad – appropriately, carrot and lettuce!

METHOD

1 Put the bread mix in a bowl with 6½–7 fl oz (185–200 ml) hand-hot water and, using a wooden spoon, mix to a dough as directed.
2 Place on a lightly floured surface and knead and stretch the dough for 5 minutes.
3 Cut into three and divide two of the thirds into 4 equal-sized pieces. Shape these 8 pieces into round bodies.
4 Divide the rest of the dough in half and from one half shape 8 round heads.

5 With the remainder of the dough make long ears and small round tails.

6 To assemble the bunnies: place the bodies well apart on the lightly oiled baking sheets and, moistening with sufficient water to join, press on the head, ears and tail (see illustration).

7 Cover the tray with a clean damp tea-towel and leave in a warm place for 35 minutes.

8 Remove the tea-towel and cook the bunnies for 15 minutes. When cooked take them off the tray with a slice and cool on a wire rack.

9 Serve with butter and salad.

Verdict from children: 'Yummy.'

Decorated eggs

Although decorated eggs are normally associated with Easter, they can be fun to paint at any time of the year.

Suggestions: show children how to paint faces on hard-boiled eggs with:

wax crayons, pencils or felt pens (of course make sure that the brand is non-toxic);

or for geometric patterns use small shiny stickers in the shape of stars or the coloured stick-on dots used to mark and number slides;

or paint designs with vegetable colourings after boiling the eggs. Warning: do not use any harmful substance like poster paints or household dyes.

TO HARD-BOIL THE EGGS

Remove the uncooked eggs from the refrigerator at least 30 minutes before needed so that they return to room temperature. It is safest for children to cover the eggs with cold water, as in the method below. If necessary, once the eggs are cooked, an adult should take the hot pan to the sink to cool the eggs under running cold water.

METHOD

1 Put eggs in a pan and cover them with cold water.
2 Bring to the boil over medium heat, reduce heat and continue to boil *gently* for 7–8 minutes.
3 Cool immediately under running cold water. This prevents an unsightly grey ring forming between yolk and white.

USES FOR HARD-BOILED EGGS

Although some children will enjoy eating eggs hard-boiled from the shells or shelled as egg mice (see page 138), others may prefer to use them in the following recipes.

Stuffed eggs

Cut the eggs in half lengthwise, carefully remove the yolks, sieve and mix with flavouring such as mayonnaise, or curry powder and mayonnaise, or mash with liver pâté. Spoon or pipe back into the hollows in the whites.

Egg sandwiches

A simple filling of eggs mashed with mayonnaise or tomato ketchup – easier to eat than egg slices.

Golden eggs

Chop the shelled hard-boiled eggs, mix with fried onions flavoured with a little dry English mustard. Serve hot on buttered toast.

Segmenting an orange

This is a suitable task for any child old enough to wield a sharp knife. It is the method my grandmother taught me for 'preparing and presenting politely' a fresh orange for dessert.

INGREDIENTS

1 small seedless orange per person

METHOD

1 Make two cuts through the skin of the orange, right round the circumference, about ¾ inch (2 cm) apart (Fig. 1).
2 Cut the peel in quarters on either side of the incisions, so that it can be cleanly removed, with the pith (Fig. 2).
3 This leaves a central 'ribbon' of peel. Find a division between two orange segments and cut through the peel at this point (Fig. 3).
4 Carefully pull the segments apart, parting more and more segments as the ribbon of peel is gently flattened (Fig. 4).
5 Serve on dessert plates. It is then only necessary for the diners to pull away each segment from the ribbon. This can be done with exquisite delicacy, without messing fingers or squirting neighbours with juice!

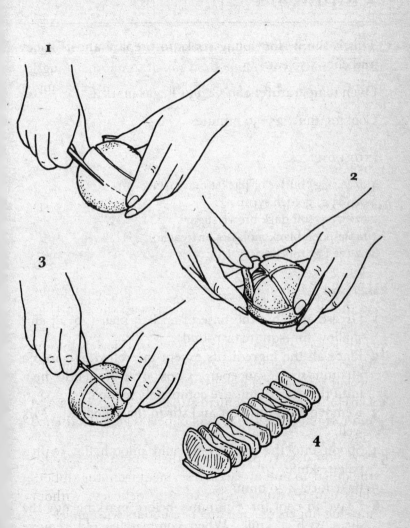

Flapjacks

This is simple for young cooks to prepare and is gooey and chewy to eat.

Oven temperature: 180°C, 350°F, gas mark 4

Cooking time: 25–30 minutes

INGREDIENTS

4 oz (115 g) butter or packet margarine
3 oz (85 g) golden syrup
2 oz (55 g) soft dark brown sugar
1 tablespoon black molasses or treacle
8 oz (225 g) rolled oats

METHOD

1 Grease and line the base of an 8–9 inch (20–23 cm) shallow tin (square or round).
2 Place all the ingredients except the rolled oats into a medium-sized saucepan. Cook over a gentle heat until the ingredients are completely melted.
3 Remove from the heat and stir in the rolled oats. Mix well.
4 Spoon into the greased tin and smooth flat with a palette knife.
5 Bake for 25–30 minutes.
6 Leave to cool for 5 minutes before marking out the slices with a knife. When completely cold remove from the baking tin and store in an airtight container.

Rock buns

This is an old-fashioned recipe, but it proved extremely popular with our taste panel and their schoolfriends.

Makes 12 buns

Oven temperature: 200°C, 400°F, gas mark 6

Cooking time: 15–20 minutes

INGREDIENTS

8 oz (225 g) plain flour
1 teaspoon baking powder
pinch ginger or mixed spice
3 oz (85 g) butter or margarine
4 oz (115 g) sugar
2 oz (55 g) currants
1 oz (30 g) sultanas
1 egg, size 3, beaten
about 1 teaspoon milk (optional)

METHOD

1 Sieve the flour, baking powder and spice. Rub in the butter or margarine.
2 Add the sugar, currants and sultanas.
3 Mix to a *stiff* dough with the egg, adding about a teaspoon of milk if necessary.
4 Use two forks to shape in rough heaps on a greased baking tray and bake for 15–20 minutes.

Fancy shaped biscuits

Oven temperature 180°C, 350°F, gas mark 4

Cooking time: 12–15 minutes

Playdoh-cutter biscuits

Make up a plain biscuit dough and let the children cut out biscuits using their (cleaned) favourite Playdoh cutters (e.g. lorries, tractors, butterflies, hearts, rabbits). This makes a robust 'non-gritty' dough, which survives the roughest treatment from three-year-olds upwards. Icing sugar gives better results than caster sugar.

INGREDIENTS

5 oz (140 g) butter or margarine
8 oz (225 g) plain flour
pinch salt
4 oz (115 g) sifted icing sugar
beaten egg to mix

METHOD

1 Rub the fat into the flour and salt.
2 Stir in the sugar and mix with beaten egg until a pliable dough is formed. Roll out and cut into shapes.
3 Bake the biscuits for 12–15 minutes.

Traffic-light biscuits

Makes 12

1 Cut large oval or round shapes from the biscuit dough.
2 With a small thimble or apple corer cut 3 holes in half the biscuits.
3 Sandwich the uncut and cut biscuits together with a thin layer of apricot jam (for easy spreading, first warm it with a little water).
4 Bake at 180°C, 350°F, gas mark 4 for 12–15 minutes. Remove from the tin and cool on a wire rack.
5 Carefully put a little blob of jam in each hole: a red jam in the top hole, more apricot in the middle, and a green jam, or lemon and lime marmalade, at the bottom to represent traffic lights.

Marion's painted biscuits

We experimented with different colours but found that red is the best colour to use.

Provide a clean paintbrush for each child.

Oven temperature: 180°C, 350°F, gas mark 4

Cooking time: 12–15 minutes

Do not use self-raising flour for this recipe: it makes the biscuits expand and that cracks the colour.

INGREDIENTS

8 oz (225 g) plain flour
pinch salt
5 oz (140 g) butter or margarine
3 oz (85 g) icing sugar
a little beaten egg to mix
2–3 egg yolks (or more for a group of children)*
red food colouring

METHOD

1 Make up the biscuit dough from the first five ingredients, roll out and cut into large fancy shapes (stars, animals, clowns or whatever appeals).
2 Beat the egg yolks, stir in drops of red food colouring and pour into saucers.
3 Let the children paint the biscuits in their chosen pattern: all over, or with spots, stripes or blobs.

* The egg whites can be used for Striped Meringues (page 143).

4 Bake for 12–15 minutes.
5 If you puncture a small hole at the top when you take them out of the oven, these painted biscuits can be hung on the Christmas tree.

Chocolate krackolates (unbaked)

Makes 9–10. These are best served in paper cases.

INGREDIENTS

1 ½ oz (45 g) butter or margarine
1 level tablespoon syrup or honey
1 ½ level tablespoons cocoa
1 level tablespoon caster sugar
2 level tablespoons desiccated coconut (optional) or 1
    teaspoon grated orange rind (optional)
1 ¼ oz (35 g) cornflakes

METHOD

1 Melt the butter and syrup slowly in a saucepan but do not allow to boil.
2 Stir in the cocoa.
3 Remove from the heat and stir in the sugar.
4 Fold in the coconut or orange rind, if used, and the cornflakes. Mix until the cornflakes are well coated.
5 Put spoonfuls into paper cases and leave in a cool place until set.

Fairy cakes

These little cup cakes are made from a basic Victoria sandwich mixture, so younger children could begin to make fairy cakes using a cake mix. With some mixes they are asked to beat up and add the eggs. When they become more skilful they can use the all-in-one method (see page 146 for Bite-sized Buns). The following recipe was used to teach seven-year-old Bethany the skills of creaming and folding in.

The plain cakes can be iced when cool with coloured glacé icing and sprinkled with hundreds and thousands.

Makes 12–16 cakes

Oven temperature: 190°C, 375°F, gas mark 5

Cooking time: 15–20 minutes

Two spoons will help to lift the mixture neatly into the paper cases.

INGREDIENTS

4 oz (115 g) soft tub margarine or butter at room
   temperature
4 oz (115 g) caster sugar
2 eggs, size 3, beaten
4 oz (115 g) self-raising flour, sifted
2 oz (55 g) sultanas *or* 2 oz (55 g) chocolate chips (optional)

METHOD

1 Preheat the oven.
2 Place the paper cases on a baking tray.
3 Cream the fat and sugar until pale and so light that when lifted up on the spoon a light tap on the side of the bowl will make the mixture fall back into the bowl. If young arms get tired from beating, a hand-held mixer helps.
4 Add the eggs a little at a time, beating well between each addition. A tablespoon of the flour can be beaten in with each egg to prevent curdling.
5 Gradually fold in the rest of the flour.
6 Fold in the sultanas or the chocolate chips if used.
7 Spoon the cake mixture into the paper cases, filling them only two thirds full to allow for rising.
8 Bake until golden, about 15–20 minutes.
9 Remove from the oven to cool on a wire rack.

Melting moments

These are biscuits simple enough for children to make for themselves with a little supervision if necessary. In the testing sessions, even three-year-old Emily participated in their preparation.

Oven temperature: 190°C, 375°F, gas mark 5

Cooking time: 15–20 minutes

INGREDIENTS

4 oz (115 g) soft tub margarine or butter at room temperature
3 oz (85 g) caster sugar
1 egg yolk
a few drops of vanilla
5 oz (140 g) self-raising flour
a few chocolate chips, polka dots or sultanas (optional)

METHOD

1 Preheat the oven. Grease a baking sheet and put to one side.
2 Cream together the butter or margarine and sugar and beat in the egg yolk.
3 Flavour with vanilla and stir in flour (and chocolate or sultanas if used) to give a stiff dough.
4 Roll the mixture into small balls and place slightly apart on the baking sheet to cook for 15–20 minutes. They melt and flatten in the oven, giving a macaroon-like finish.

Chocolate-dipped fruit

This keeps the children usefully occupied before a dinner party (but it is messy, so supply aprons). In summer one otherwise indulgent grandmother protects her kitchen by setting up the work table for the chocolate dipping in the shade out of doors.

Choose firm, clean fruit to avoid having to wash and squash it. Depending on the age of the children, you may have to supervise the melting of the chocolate.

INGREDIENTS

plain chocolate
strawberries, cherries *or* glacé pineapple

METHOD

1 Melt the chocolate either in a microwave or in a bowl over gently simmering water. Do not overheat.
2 Pick up the fruit by the stem or the edge and dip it into the chocolate, lifting it up so that surplus chocolate drips back into the bowl.
3 Stand the dipped fruit on lightly oiled kitchen foil placed on a plate that can be kept in the refrigerator until served to your guests.

Witches' cake

Here is a recipe sent from a New Zealand trained dietitian, my co-worker for many years, Dr Diane Holdsworth-Katrios. This is a Greek vegan cake, adapted with the help of Matia, her daughter, for witches, wizards and magicians. The cooked cake has a moist, solid texture, and is very good.

Oven temperature: 180°C, 350°F, gas mark 4

Cooking time: 1 ¼ – 1 ½ hours

INGREDIENTS

1 mug orange juice or apple juice
1 mug corn oil
1 small mug sugar*
½ teaspoon grated orange peel
1 teaspoon cinnamon
1 mug washed sultanas
1 mug chopped walnuts
3 ½ mugs self-raising flour
caster sugar for dusting

METHOD

1 *First make the Brew*: into the cauldron put 1 mug water, and the juice and oil.

---

* Use white or brown sugar – brown makes better mud later in the recipe.

2 *Next prepare the Dry Mixture*: in another bowl, mix the sugar, peel, cinnamon, sultanas and walnuts.

3 *Now make the Magic Mud Mixture*: recite the following while you add the Dry Mixture to the Brew:

> Abracadabra,
> This cake for you,
> Has no slugs or snails
> Just mud in the brew.

4 Let this wet mud sit for a while after stirring, and get on with the next things to do:
(a) Turn on the oven to 180°C, 350°F, gas mark 4.
(b) Line a big cake tin, about 10 inches, *twice* with greaseproof paper and brush with corn oil.

5 *When the oven is hot, make the Glorious Mud*: to the Magic Mud Mixture in the cauldron, add the self-raising flour. Quickly stir the cauldron full of Glorious Mud until well mixed.

6 Pour the mixture into the cake tin. Cover with a sheet of greaseproof paper and cook for 1¼–1½ hours.

7 After cooking, leave to stand for 15–20 minutes before turning out on to a wire rack. Sprinkle with a little caster sugar.

Serving hint: Cut in thin and thick slices and ask witch size is wanted!

Marshmallow sticks

Children can make these for a charity bazaar. They are an attractive, inexpensive purchase and a welcome nibble for bazaar visitors.

INGREDIENTS

pink and white marshmallows
glacé cherries (red or mixed colours)
cocktail sticks

METHOD

1 Spear a white marshmallow on to a cocktail stick, followed by a glacé cherry and finally a pink marshmallow.
2 Arrange these in a circle on a plate. Put another plate by the side to collect the discarded cocktail sticks.

Chapter Five
Recipes from Holidays

STARTERS

Feta cheese starter (Greece)
French onion soup
Garlic bread
Gazpacho (Spain)

SALADS AND VEGETABLES

Carrot raita (India)
Couscous (Middle East)
Indian fried potatoes
Danish red cabbage (sweet-sour)
Peas in the French fashion
Raw mushroom salad (Scandinavia)
Ratatouille bake

FISH

Herrings in oatmeal with Scotch whisky
Jansson's temptation (Sweden)
Smoked salmon and cream-cheese bagels (Israel)
Steamed fish in pink sauce (Norway)
Tuna or salmon niçoise

MEAT

Danish meat cakes

DESSERTS

Danish 'peasant girl with veil'
Hot fruit salad (New Zealand)
Rød grød (Scandinavia)
Louisiana bread pudding
    whisky sauce
Norwegian apple cake
Tarte des demoiselles Tatin (French upside-down apple
    tart)
Tiramisu (Italy)
Vanilla sauce (Norway)

Feta cheese starter (Greece)

This makes a tasty alternative to *taramosalata*. It is also suitable for a dip for cut-up raw vegetables.

Serves 4–6

INGREDIENTS

2 oz (55 g) firm white bread without crusts
5 oz (140 g) feta cheese*
1 clove garlic peeled and finely crushed *or* 1 tablespoon
   finely grated onion *or* chopped spring onion
2 tablespoons lemon juice
freshly ground black pepper
approx. 3 fl oz (85 ml) olive oil
4–6 tablespoons Greek yogurt
for garnish: black olives

Serve with crackers or water biscuits.

METHOD

1 Soak the bread in cold water for several minutes. Squeeze as dry as possible and discard the water.
2 Put all the ingredients, except the oil and yogurt, into a food processor.
3 Process, pouring in the oil gradually to make a smooth paste. *If using a blender* put in the cheese, lemon juice and oil alternately with the squeezed bread.
4 Add the yogurt and beat to a thick consistency.

* If the cheese tastes too salty, first soak it in a little milk and then lift out and drain dry.

French onion soup

Serves 3–4 (will freeze)

INGREDIENTS

2 large onions (*not* the mild Spanish type)
1 clove garlic, finely sliced
1 oz (30 g) margarine
salt and pepper
2 teaspoons flour
pinch of caster sugar
1 pint (565 ml) beef stock
3–4 thick slices French bread
French mustard
grated cheese (preferably Gruyère)

METHOD

1 Peel the onions, cut in half and slice finely.
2 Melt the margarine in a large saucepan, add the onion and garlic slices and cook over a moderate heat, stirring frequently to prevent burning, until golden brown. (This could take from 15–30 minutes according to the depth of colour you prefer.)
3 Stir in the seasoning, flour and sugar and cook for 1 minute.
4 Gradually add the stock, bring to the boil, cover and simmer for 20–25 minutes until the onions are tender.
5 Lightly spread one side of the bread with French

mustard* and top thickly with grated cheese. Grill until the cheese is melted and beginning to brown.

6 Serve the hot soup in warmed deep soup bowls with the grilled French bread floating on top.

Garlic bread

INGREDIENTS

1 clove garlic
2–3 oz (55–85 g) butter
½ teaspoon mixed dried herbs or 1 teaspoon fresh herbs
1 small stick French bread

METHOD

1 Squeeze the garlic through a garlic press and add to the melted butter and the herbs (it can be melted and mixed in a bowl in a microwave).
2 Slice the French loaf and dunk one side of each slice into the garlic butter.
3 Parcel the reassembled loaf in usable quantities in foil and refrigerate or freeze until needed.
4 Reheat in a hot oven for about 10 minutes before serving. *From frozen*: reheat at 180°C, 350°F, gas mark 4 for 15 minutes; turn back foil and heat for a further 10 minutes at 230°C, 450°F, gas mark 8 to crisp and brown.

* To make it easier to cut through the French bread with a soup spoon, it helps if the outside crust only of the bread is gashed down at intervals with a sharp knife before spreading.

Gazpacho (Spain)

This is quickly made in a food processor.

Serves 2

INGREDIENTS

half cucumber, unpeeled
quarter green and/or red pepper
small wedge of onion
1 can (14 oz, 400 g) tomatoes
2 tablespoons olive oil
¾ tablespoon wine vinegar
pinch of cayenne pepper
salt and pepper

Can be served with Garlic Bread (see previous recipe).

METHOD

1 Cut the unpeeled cucumber in thick chunks. Remove seeds from the peppers.
2 Process the cucumber, peppers and onion for a few seconds until finely chopped.
3 Pour in the tomatoes and juice. Add the oil, vinegar and seasonings. Process again for a few seconds.
4 Taste for seasoning. Serve cold.

Note: this can also be made in a liquidizer. Simply blend all the ingredients together for a few seconds. This gives a smoother texture. Try it also as a speedy sauce to accompany meat loaf or fishcakes.

Carrot raita (India)

Carrot Raita makes a refreshing summer salad.

INGREDIENTS

Per portion
1 small carrot, peeled and grated
3 tablespoons natural yogurt
fresh mint, chopped
pinch of sugar
pinch of nutmeg or cumin
salt and pepper

METHOD

1 Stir the grated carrot into the yogurt.
2 Stir in plenty of chopped mint and season to taste.

Couscous (Middle East)

This is particularly enjoyable with chicken curry or steamed fish, or can be served as a vegetable on its own.

Serves 2

INGREDIENTS

2 oz (55 g) couscous
1 large spring onion
2 oz (55 g) mushrooms
¼ green pepper
1 stick celery
1 oz (30 g) mange-touts
dash of soy sauce
seasoning: ginger, pepper and salt *or* garlic salt
parsley to garnish

METHOD

1 Just cover the couscous with boiling water and leave to swell slightly for 10 minutes.
2 Simmer with the sliced vegetables until cooked (approximately 10–15 minutes).
3 Add a dash of soy sauce, season with ginger, pepper and salt or garlic salt and garnish with chopped parsley.

Indian fried potatoes

A spicy side dish to serve hot with curry and rice.
It is best cooked in a non-stick frying-pan.

Serves 2

Cooking time: 5–10 minutes

INGREDIENTS

1 large potato
1 ½ tablespoons oil
⅓ teaspoon chilli powder*
⅓ teaspoon turmeric powder
⅓ teaspoon salt

METHOD

1 Peel the potato and cut in cubes (roughly ¾ inch, 2 cm). Wash through a sieve.
2 Heat the oil in a frying-pan. When hot, lightly fry the chilli powder, turmeric and salt.
3 Add the raw, drained potato cubes, stir, cover and let them cook in the oil until lightly browned (shake and turn the cubes occasionally during the cooking).

* Mild or strong according to choice.

Danish red cabbage (sweet-sour)

This recipe brings back memories of a family holiday in Denmark and an invited tour around the Plumrose factory. Our young daughters stood enthralled by the sight of the sausages popping out of the machines – not even the lure of lunch at the Tivoli gardens could drag them away! The Plumrose cookery expert's recipe is adapted below for smaller quantities – and it is excellent served with sausages . . .

Sweet-sour red cabbage can be prepared several days before it is required and in fact improves with keeping.

Serves 4

Cooking time: 1–1 ½ hours

INGREDIENTS

½ small red cabbage (about 1 lb, 450 g)
1 large cooking apple
1 oz (30 g) butter
4 fl oz (115 ml) wine vinegar
4 oz (115 g) demerara sugar
generous pinch of powdered cloves
salt and ground black pepper
3 large tablespoons redcurrant jelly

METHOD

1 Shred the cabbage, wash and drain. Peel, core and coarsely grate the apple.
2 Melt the butter in a saucepan and add the cabbage and apple. Stir to coat.
3 Add the vinegar, 6 fl oz (170 ml) water, sugar and cloves, put the lid on the pan and cook very slowly over gentle heat until tender, stirring occasionally and adding more water if necessary.
4 Season with salt and pepper, add the redcurrant jelly and continue cooking for 15 minutes. Taste for sweet-sour flavour, adding more redcurrant jelly if needed. Serve hot.

Peas in the French fashion

Because fresh peas in the pod have only a short season, I have adapted one of my favourite recipes to use frozen garden peas, the larger variety, not petits pois.

Serves 4

INGREDIENTS

1 bunch salad onions, white part only, *or* 4 pickling onions, halved, *or* 2 small onions, quartered
knob of butter
1 lump of sugar (or ½ teaspoon)
1 small round lettuce
salt and pepper
12 oz (340 g) frozen garden peas
1–2 teaspoons butter
1–2 teaspoons flour

METHOD

1 Toss the onions in the butter for a few minutes to soften without browning.
2 Add 2 tablespoons water, the sugar and the lettuce, cut into eight, washed well and lifted dripping wet into the pan. Season and cook for 5 minutes.
3 Add the peas; heat to defrost. Simmer for 3 minutes.
4 With a spoon, make a paste of the butter and flour, then drop it bit by bit into the pan, stirring until the liquor thickens. Taste for seasoning.
5 Serve the peas with the onion, lettuce and thickened liquor.

Raw mushroom salad (Scandinavia)

INGREDIENTS

a small handful of button mushrooms for each person

For the vinaigrette (sufficient for 1–4 portions)
2 tablespoons wine vinegar
4–6 tablespoons oil
1 teaspoon sugar
½ crushed clove of garlic (optional)
salt and black pepper

To serve with fish
peeled diced cucumber

To serve with hot or cold meat
chopped watercress and chicory

METHOD

1 Shake or beat all the vinaigrette ingredients together. (Use the greater quantity of oil if you prefer a bland rather than a sharp dressing.) Taste for flavour.
2 Slice or quarter the mushrooms and marinade them in the vinaigrette for 2–3 hours.*
3 Add the chosen salad vegetables.

* The mushrooms may be marinaded overnight. This makes the salad darker in colour and the mushrooms softer in texture but this is often preferred when it is to be served with hot food.

Ratatouille bake

Serves 4 (or 2 servings one day and the rest frozen for another time)

Oven temperature: 190°C, 375°F, gas mark 5

Cooking time: 40 minutes on top of the stove and a further 15–20 minutes in the oven

INGREDIENTS

1 large onion, peeled and sliced
4 tablespoons oil (olive or sunflower)
1 medium green pepper, de-seeded and sliced
½ small red pepper, de-seeded and sliced
1 medium aubergine, diced
2 courgettes, sliced
small can (8 oz, 225 g) chopped tomatoes
salt and freshly ground black pepper
chopped fresh basil or parsley (optional)

For topping, to serve 2
6 tablespoons Greek yogurt
1 tablespoon milk
1 egg, beaten

METHOD

1 In a flameproof casserole with lid, sauté the onion gently in oil until softened.
2 Add the peppers and aubergine and sauté for a few minutes.

3 Add the courgettes, stir in and leave the mixture to cook, still covered with the lid, for 5 minutes or so, stirring occasionally.

4 Stir in the tomatoes with their juice, season, add herbs and simmer covered for at least another 30 minutes.*

5 Beat together the yogurt, milk and egg. Pour over the ratatouille mixture and transfer to the oven to bake uncovered for 15–20 minutes until set.

Speedy alternative: use a pack of shop-bought frozen ratatouille, and reheat according to the instructions before adding the topping and baking.

* After step 4, the cooked ratatouille mixture can be frozen in a freezer-to-oven container. Reheat from frozen. Add the topping once the mixture is heated through, and continue baking at 190°C, 375°F, gas mark 5 for 15–20 minutes to set.

Herrings in oatmeal with Scotch whisky

This brings back the memory of a holiday in the Scottish isles. The sadness of leaving was gladdened by a stop-off in Inverness to catch the homeward train: herrings flambéed in whisky were on the menu for 'a taste of Scotland'. This is how I think they may have cooked them.

Serves 1

INGREDIENTS

1 fresh herring, cleaned, with the backbone removed*
2–3 tablespoons coarse oatmeal *or* 2–3 tablespoons quick porridge oats
½ teaspoon salt
fat for shallow frying
1 tablespoon Scotch whisky

Garnish with watercress or tomato wedges and eat with crusty bread rolls.

* A fishmonger will do this for you, or you may buy them already boned. To do it yourself, remove the head, scrape off the scales from tail to head, slit along the belly to remove the roe (can be fried with the fish) and clean out the innards. Place the opened fish skin side uppermost on a board and press firmly all the way along the centre back. Turn the fish over and ease the bone away from the flesh. Cut off the tail and fins.

METHOD

1 Wash the fish and pat dry. Coat all over with the oatmeal/oats and salt, mixed together, pressing on well.
2 Fry in hot fat, about 5 minutes on each side.
3 Pour off excess fat, add the whisky to the pan (it will splutter), strike a long match and flame off the alcohol, but not the flavour.

Jansson's temptation (Sweden)

This is a popular informal party dish, served late at night with beer, rye bread or dark crispbread, and cheese.

Serves 4 (quantities may be increased for more guests)

Oven temperature: 200°C, 400°F, gas mark 6 for 30 minutes; then 150°C, 300°F, gas mark 2 for a further 30 minutes

INGREDIENTS

1 onion, sliced
1 oz (30 g) butter
2 medium-sized raw potatoes
small tin (50 g) anchovy fillets
1 small carton (5 fl oz, 140 ml) single cream

METHOD

1 Fry the onion gently in a knob of the butter until softened but not brown.
2 Peel the potatoes and slice lengthwise in thin slices (if too thick they will not 'melt' together in the cooking).
3 Into a well-buttered baking dish place layers of potato, onion and halved anchovy fillets, finishing with a layer of potatoes.

4 Moisten with a little of the anchovy oil and dot with the remaining butter.

5 Bake at 200°C, 400°F, gas mark 6 for 10 minutes.

6 Add half the cream and bake for a further 10 minutes.

7 Add the rest of the cream and bake for another 10 minutes.

8 Reduce the heat to 150°C, 300°F, gas mark 2 and bake for a final 30 minutes. The potatoes need to be soft but crisped on top. Serve hot from the baking dish.

Smoked salmon and cream-cheese bagels (Israel)

Bagels are now quite readily available. (Bagels are boiled and baked rolls with a hole in the centre and a smooth hard shiny surface.) Ordinary poppy seed rolls could be substituted, but not if you want the authentic recipe.

INGREDIENTS

bagels (1 per serving but this depends on appetite)
softened butter
cream cheese
sliced smoked salmon
freshly ground black pepper
fresh lemon
black olives

METHOD

1 Slice the freshly bought bagels across in half. If you wish, they can be heated for a few moments in a hot oven.
2 Spread each half sparingly with the butter and thickly with the cream cheese.
3 Arrange smoked salmon on top, season with a little black pepper and a squeeze of lemon juice. Serve garnished with black olives.

Steamed fish in pink sauce (Norway)

Serves 2

INGREDIENTS

½ lb (225 g) fillet of cod or haddock, skinned
2–3 tablespoons milk
4 tablespoons crème fraîche or sour cream
1 tablespoon red 'caviar' from cod*
freshly ground black pepper
boiled potatoes

METHOD

1 Steam the fish in 2–3 tablespoons milk (it can be cooked from frozen).
2 Warm the crème fraîche and 'caviar' in a small jug placed in a saucepan of hot water. Season with pepper (no salt because it is already salty). Add a little liquid from the fish.
3 Serve the hot fish with this pink sauce and boiled potatoes.

* Can be bought in small pots at the delicatessen.

Tuna or salmon niçoise

Serves 2

INGREDIENTS

crunchy lettuce
canned tuna (or cooked fresh salmon), flaked
1–2 hard-boiled eggs, quartered
1 oz (30 g) black olives
2 oz (55 g) cooked or canned French beans
1–2 tomatoes, sliced or cut into wedges
slices of red pepper (optional)
½ small can anchovy fillets, halved
French dressing
garlic croûtons *or* crusty French bread

METHOD

1 Make a bed of lettuce and arrange the next seven
  ingredients on it.
2 Just before serving pour on the dressing. Top with
  the croûtons or serve with slices of French bread.

Danish meat cakes

The use of soda water may come as a surprise, but it gives a soft light texture.

Serves 4

INGREDIENTS

1 egg
8 oz (225 g) minced beef or veal
8 oz (225 g) minced pork
1 large onion, finely chopped
4 oz (115 g) fresh white breadcrumbs
salt and pepper
8 fl oz (225 ml) bottle soda water
2 oz (55 g) butter
2 tablespoons oil

Serve with boiled potatoes, and Danish Red Cabbage (page 180), Beetroot and Orange (page 283) or sliced beetroot.

METHOD

1 Beat the egg in the mixing bowl and fork in the meats, onion, breadcrumbs, seasoning and soda water. Mix well.
2 Cover and chill for 1 hour.
3 Shape into 8 oblong meat cakes about 2 × 4 inches (5 × 10 cm). They should be ¾ inch (2 cm) thick.
4 In a large frying-pan heat the butter and oil and fry the meat cakes over medium heat until cooked and browned, about 8 minutes on each side.
5 Drain on kitchen paper.

Danish 'peasant girl with veil'

For this adapted recipe I use wholemeal bread instead of white and omit the usual butter for frying the crumbs. The traditional recipe uses a thick apple purée but my cousin Gill recommends strawberries or peaches when they are in season and layers them with thick yogurt or fromage frais instead of the traditional cream. Serve in a glass bowl or in individual glasses so that the layers are visible.

Serves 4–5

Oven temperature: 190°C, 375°F, gas mark 5 to caramelize the crumbs for 15–20 minutes

INGREDIENTS

5 large slices wholemeal bread, in crumbs*
5 tablespoons demerara sugar*
1 rounded teaspoon cinnamon*
Greek-style yogurt *or* fromage frais
1 punnet strawberries, *or* 3 peaches *or* other chosen fruit
a few tablespoons liqueur, e. g. Grand Marnier (optional)

* Note: I recommend you make more than you need of the caramelized crumbs and store the surplus in the refrigerator. They will keep, tightly covered, for several weeks.

METHOD

1 Mix crumbs, sugar and cinnamon. Spread on a baking sheet. Heat in the oven, stirring occasionally until caramelized to a golden brown. Cool.
2 Meanwhile slice the strawberries or peaches and sprinkle with liqueur.
3 Put layers of fruit, yogurt or fromage frais, and caramelized crumbs into the bowl, ending with a sprinkling of crumbs.

Hot fruit salad

This recipe was given to me by a New Zealander. As they happily eat Christmas pudding on a sunny beach in December, I agreed to try a hot fruit salad in the cold of England! Different – and delicious.

The fruit salad is first heated on top of the stove. Serve hot straight away, or transfer it to a fondue dish and keep it warm over a spirit lamp at the table before serving.

INGREDIENTS

1 can of lichees
1 can of guavas
white wine (optional)
oranges
peaches/nectarines
pears
kiwi fruit
apples
kirsch

METHOD

1 Heat the lichees in the juices from the cans, plus white wine if used, and any juice from the chopped oranges.
2 When the lichees and juices are hot, stir in all the peeled and cut up fruits.
3 Before serving, stir in a few tablespoons of kirsch.

Rød grød (Scandinavia)

INGREDIENTS

½ lb (225 g) redcurrants
sugar to taste
potato flour or arrowroot for thickening
single cream for serving

METHOD

1 Stew the redcurrants with ¾ pint (425 ml) water
   until the fruit softens and the juices run.
2 Strain off the juice into a measuring jug.
3 Return to the pan and sweeten to taste.
4 Allow approximately 1½ tablespoons of potato flour
   or arrowroot to thicken every ¾ pint (425 ml) juice
   (first mixing to a thin cream with a little water, then
   stirring vigorously into the heated fruit juice).
5 Pour into the serving bowl. Sprinkle the surface with
   sugar and allow to cool before serving with single
   cream.

Louisiana bread pudding

Bread pudding is usually reckoned to be the frugal housewife's answer to leftover stale bread. But in New Orleans, Louisiana, I found it transformed into the house speciality on most local menus, soft in texture, bursting with dried pecan nuts and dried fruit, and served with a heady whisky sauce.

Use any stale bread, but for the authentic Louisiana texture, attack stale French bread with a rolling-pin to crush it into coarse crumbs; and try to find pecan nuts, although walnuts can be substituted.

As a guide I have detailed the ingredients and suggested the quantities, but this is a flexible recipe: vary it according to the dried fruits and nuts available in your store cupboard.

You will need a well-buttered baking dish. This pudding freezes well, so you may prefer to use a dish suitable both for oven and freezer.

Oven temperature: 180°C, 350°F, gas mark 4 (but there is no need to preheat the oven)

Cooking time: about 1 ¼ hours

INGREDIENTS

6–8 oz (170–225 g) stale bread
4 oz (115 g) sugar
2 oz (55 g) raisins/ mixed dried fruit
1–2 tablespoons desiccated coconut
2 oz (55 g) chopped pecans/ walnuts
½ level teaspoon cinnamon

½ level teaspoon nutmeg
approx. ½ pint (285 ml) milk
1 egg, beaten
few drops vanilla essence
1 oz (30 g) melted butter

METHOD

1 Crumble the bread.
2 In a large bowl, combine all the dry ingredients.
3 Mix to a soft consistency with the milk, egg, vanilla
  and melted butter.
4 Place in the oven and bake for about 1¼ hours until
  the top is golden brown. Serve warm with whisky
  sauce.

Whisky sauce

For a richer sauce, make Vanilla Sauce (p. 206) and
stir in the whisky before serving.

INGREDIENTS

1 cup milk
1 tablespoon sugar
2 teaspoons cornflour
3–4 fl oz (85–115 ml) whisky (preferably Bourbon) or
  brandy

METHOD

1 Scald the milk with the sugar.
2 Mix the cornflour with the cold whisky or brandy
  and add to the milk.
3 Bring to the boil and simmer until thick.

Norwegian apple cake

This is best served on the day of making, but can be
slightly re-warmed if eaten later. It also freezes well: cut
into portions and freeze uncovered on foil-lined baking
sheets. When firm, pack in freezer film in a polythene
container. Defrost and re-warm before serving.

Serves 10–12

Oven temperature: 200°C, 400°F, gas mark 6

Cooking time: 20–25 minutes

You will need a shallow roasting-tin approximately 12
× 9½ inches (30 × 24 cm). Butter and flour the tin
before use.

INGREDIENTS

2–3 Bramley cooking apples
2 eggs, size 3
8 oz (225 g) caster sugar
scant 4 oz (105 g) butter
just over ¼ pint (150 ml) creamy milk
6½ oz (185 g) plain flour
2 rounded teaspoons baking powder

METHOD

1 Peel, core and slice the quartered apples thinly into
wedges about ¼ inch (½ cm) thick. Set aside but
proceed with the next steps immediately to avoid discoloration.

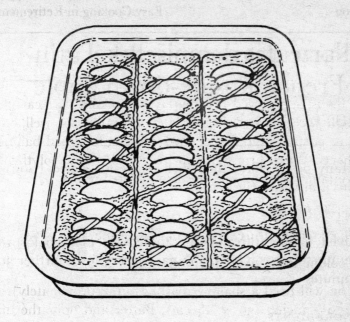

2 Whisk eggs and sugar together thoroughly until foamy and creamy.

3 Put butter and milk into a small pan and bring to the boil. Stir the boiling liquid into the whisked eggs and sugar.

4 Gradually and carefully fold in the sifted flour and baking powder. Do this lightly with a large spoon, to make a smooth batter.

5 Pour into the prepared tin.

6 Arrange the apple wedges in close rows, covering the batter. Sprinkle with more caster sugar.

7 Bake for 20–25 minutes until risen and golden.

8 Allow to cool in the tin before cutting into diamonds or squares.

Tarte des demoiselles Tatin (French upside-down apple tart)

Many people have their own recipe for Tarte Tatin – this is my favourite version.

Serves 6

Oven temperature: 200°C, 400°F, gas mark 6 for 10 minutes and 190°C, 375°F, gas mark 5 for a further 30 minutes

INGREDIENTS

½ oz (15 g) soft butter
2 oz (55 g) caster sugar
¼ teaspoon cinnamon

Pastry
a scant 3 oz (80 g) butter
5 oz (140 g) self-raising flour
2 teaspoons caster sugar

Apple mixture
2 lb (1 kg) baking apples
2 oz (55 g) caster sugar
¼ teaspoon cinnamon
2 oz (55 g) melted butter

METHOD

1 You will need a round ovenproof soufflé or baking dish about 2½ inches (6 cm) deep and 7 inches (18 cm) in diameter. Butter it well, particularly the base, and sprinkle thickly with a mixture of 2 oz (55 g) caster sugar and ¼ teaspoon cinnamon.

2 Make the pastry by rubbing the butter lightly into the flour and the 2 teaspoons sugar and mixing to a dough with water.

3 Peel, core and cut the apples in thin wedges of approximately ⅛ inch (3 mm) thick.

4 Place a layer of apples in the dish. Mix the rest of the sugar and cinnamon together and sprinkle some of the mixture over the apples; pour on a little of the melted butter.

5 Repeat these layers, finishing with a layer of apple.

6 Roll out the pastry ⅛ inch (¼ cm) thick to fit the top of the dish, allowing the edges to fall inside.

7 Bake at 200°C, 400°F, gas mark 6 for the first 10 minutes, lowering the heat to 190°C, 375°F, gas mark 5 for a further 30 minutes.

8 Carefully turn out upside down on to a serving plate. If the apples are not quite brown enough, sprinkle with icing sugar and put under the grill.

9 Serve warm. It may be reheated, covered, in a moderate oven for 20 minutes.

Tiramisu (Italy)

This is a rich mixture; half quantities can be made. Mascarpone cheese may be found at Italian delicatessens, and other specialist cheese counters. I have found it in 500 g and 250 g tubs.

Serves 10

For this quantity, you will need an oblong china or glass dish, approximately 7 × 12 in (18 × 30 cm).

INGREDIENTS

large mug of strong black coffee
2 tablespoons rum
yolks of 4 eggs and the whites of 2
4 oz (115 g) sugar
500 g (18 oz) Mascarpone cheese
24 lady fingers or boudoir biscuits (sponge fingers)
2 tablespoons Drambuie, Grand Marnier or brandy
cocoa powder

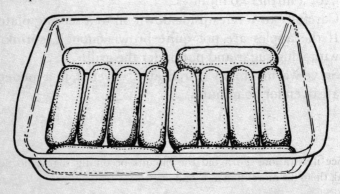

METHOD

1 Add the rum to the coffee and allow to get cold.
2 Whisk the 4 yolks of eggs with the sugar and add the cheese.
3 Add the Drambuie or Grand Marnier or brandy to this cheese mixture.
4 Whisk the egg whites and fold in.
5 Pour the coffee and rum mixture into a shallow plate; briefly dip the biscuits into it and use them to layer the bottom of the dish.* Add half the cheese mixture, and then another layer of dipped biscuits and the rest of the cheese.
6 Sieve cocoa powder over the top and put in the fridge until the next day.

* See illustration. To avoid the biscuits becoming soggy, do not soak them for more than a second or two.

Vanilla sauce (Norway)

Vanilla Sauce is often served in Norway with redcurrants or other stewed fruit. The popular thickening agent in Scandinavia is potato flour, but if you cannot find this in your shops, substitute cornflour.

With double the quantity of potato flour or cornflour, it can be made thicker and used as a cake filling.

Serves 3

INGREDIENTS

6 fl oz (170 ml) milk
½ tablespoon sugar
¼ tablespoon vanilla sugar*
1 small egg
1 teaspoon potato flour or cornflour
1 tablespoon whipped cream (use double or whipping cream)

METHOD

1 Scald the milk with the sugar.
2 Add to the beaten egg, return to the pan and gently bring just to the boil.
3 Thicken with the potato flour or cornflour, mixed to a thin cream with a little water.
4 When cold stir in the whipped cream.

* Keep some caster sugar with a vanilla pod in a tightly stoppered jar. Alternatively, use a total of ¾ tablespoon sugar and beat in a few drops of vanilla essence with the egg.

Chapter Six
Breakfasts

Fresh citrus juice
Oatmeal porridge
Ten-minute dried-fruit compote
Red apple muesli
Fruit and nut bowl
Carrot and apple muffins
Kippers
Baked French toast
Three-fruit marmalade
Seville orange marmalade (using a processor or liquid-
    izer)
Evelyn's wholemeal bread
Breakfast or brunch ideas from holidays

Recipes in this chapter are shown in bold type.

For those who tend to wake up *during* breakfast, I suggest a simple starter such as canned grapefruit segments with canned figs or prunes; **Fresh Citrus Juice** could be prepared the night before (immediate consumption is best, but it can be stored overnight in a covered glass in the refrigerator). Late risers may also appreciate ideas for a **Danish Brunch** (page 224).

For the early risers, there is the joy of segmenting fresh oranges and grapefruit, simmering a tangy **Dried Fruit Compote**, or preparing **Baked French Toast** or **Carrot and Apple Muffins**. Or they can enjoy the taste of **Kippers** or poached smoked haddock.

Those who still appreciate the Great British Breakfast will enjoy **Porridge**, eggs and bacon, kedgeree, kidneys, regional sausages and black pudding, mushrooms and, of course, rolls or **Home-baked Bread**, and chunky **Home-made Marmalade**.

But nowadays perhaps the majority of us have switched to breakfast cereals/yogurt regimes (see my recipes for **Red Apple Muesli** and **Fruit and Nut Bowl**, which are variations on this theme).

Do you prefer just tea, toast and marmalade? In retirement, you may still like to recognize the weekend with a two-day change to buttery croissants and preserves, served with coffee or hot chocolate.

Are you more adventurous about breakfast on holidays? Back home, my mind boggles at some of the food combinations (given at the end of this chapter) that I have tackled on trips abroad – sausages, waffles and maple syrup? pickled herrings and radishes? . . . delicious!

Fresh citrus juice

There is nothing to match the flavour of freshly squeezed citrus juice.

Suggested combinations for freshly squeezed juices

For about 2 servings use

3–4 small juicy oranges;

or 1 grapefruit (white, pink or ruby);

or 2 small juicy oranges, ½ grapefruit and ½ lemon;

or ½ pink grapefruit and 1–2 medium oranges;

or 4 small red 'blood oranges'.

Look for firm fruit, with a bright shiny skin and small pores. Soft, spongy fruit, with large pores far apart, indicates a thick peel. Avoid citrus fruit with hard, leathery skin: the fruit may be old and the flavour and quality impaired. But small marks or blemishes on the skin are not important, unless you want to grate the rind; they are caused by the weather and do not reflect the condition of the fruit. Choose citrus fruit that feels heavy for its size, because that should be a sign of juiciness.

Oatmeal porridge

This recipe uses oatmeal as a change from porridge oats.

Serves 1

INGREDIENTS

2 tablespoons fine oatmeal
1 tablespoon pinhead oatmeal
¼–½ teaspoon salt
1 extra teaspoon fine oatmeal
serve with full-cream milk

METHOD

1 Soak the 3 tablespoons oatmeal and the salt in 7½ fl oz (215 ml) water overnight in a small saucepan.
2 Next morning bring slowly to the boil, stirring, and continue to stir until it thickens (about 2 minutes).
3 Serve immediately, sprinkled with a little dry fine oatmeal and with full-cream milk to pour around the dish.

My Scottish friends would be horrified if I suggested serving porridge with demerara sugar – perhaps, like me, you can be won over to porridge without sugar.

Ten-minute dried-fruit compote

A mixture of dried fruits can be bought in packets, ready for soaking overnight and cooking with water and brown sugar the next day. But I prefer the juiciness and full flavour of the no-soak dried fruits, nowadays often sold at greengrocers, health food shops and supermarkets.

4–5 servings; or make half quantities

INGREDIENTS

10 oz (285 g) stoned ready-to-eat prunes
5 oz (140 g) dried no-soak apricots
5 oz (140 g) dried ready-to-eat figs
2–3 thin slivers of orange rind
serve with yogurt (optional)

METHOD

1 Wash off the powdery surface (generally potato flour) from the figs. Place all the fruit in a saucepan with ½ pint (285 ml) cold water. Add slivers of orange rind, shaved from a scrubbed orange with a potato peeler.
2 Bring to the boil, cover and simmer for 5–10 minutes. Serve warm or refrigerate. It keeps for several days.

Red apple muesli

This is my version of the famous Swiss Dr Bircher-Benner muesli, formulated for his patients' health. The yogurt adds more nourishment and the red skin of the apple gives it extra eye appeal.

INGREDIENTS

For each serving
1 red-skinned apple
juice of half a lemon
1 tablespoon porridge oats
2–3 tablespoons low-fat unsweetened natural yogurt
clear honey to taste
2 teaspoons roughly chopped nuts
optional: add extra cut up seasonal fruits (this can turn it
    from a breakfast dish into a more substantial lunch)

METHOD

1 Coarsely grate the washed unpeeled apple into the serving bowl.
2 Stir in the lemon juice immediately to prevent discoloration.
3 Add the oats, yogurt, honey and nuts, tasting for flavour. (I like it refreshingly sharp and lemony, but others may prefer the soothing flavour of the honey.)

Fruit and nut bowl

Serves 2

INGREDIENTS

5 fl oz (140 ml) natural low-fat yogurt
½–1 oz (15–30 g) mixed chopped nuts *or* hazelnuts chopped
  or finely crushed
¼ teaspoon ground cinnamon
1 banana, sliced
1 orange, peeled and segmented
a few spoonfuls of Sultana Bran or Bran Flakes mixed with a
  few raisins

METHOD

1 Mix together the yogurt, nuts and cinnamon. Stir in
  the banana and orange.
2 Sprinkle generously with the Sultana Bran or Bran
  Flakes and raisins.

Carrot and apple muffins

This recipe comes from *Commonsense Nutrition for Seniors* (Ministry of Agriculture and Food, Consumer Information Centre, Ontario, Canada).

If you like muffins for breakfast it is worth investing in a muffin tin. This can be non-stick or can be used in conjunction with cake or muffin papers.

Makes 6–8 muffins

Oven temperature: 180°C, 350°F, gas mark 4

Cooking time: 20–25 minutes

INGREDIENTS

6 oz (170 g) plain flour, unsifted
¾ teaspoon baking powder
¼ teaspoon bicarbonate of soda
¼ teaspoon cinnamon
2 oz (55 g) sugar
2 fl oz (55 ml) vegetable oil
1 egg, beaten
½ teaspoon vanilla essence
1 medium carrot, peeled and grated
1 peeled, cored and quartered medium cooking apple, stewed
   or ¼ cup (2 fl oz) apple sauce *

* This can be bought in a jar or can, but is easy to make by stewing 1 peeled, cored and quartered medium cooking apple in the minimum of water until thoroughly softened and fluffy.

METHOD

1 Combine the flour, baking powder, bicarbonate of soda, cinnamon and sugar in a mixing bowl.
2 In a measuring jug beat the vegetable oil with the egg and vanilla and add the carrot and apple sauce.
3 Add the moist ingredients to the dry, stirring until just mixed.
4 Spoon this batter into the greased muffin tins, or tins lined with papers.
5 Bake for 20–25 minutes, until golden.

These are best eaten fresh but they can be stored in an airtight container in a cool place for a day or two.

Kippers

In response to consumer demand, it is now easier to obtain undyed kippers, pale in colour but fully mellow in flavour. Kippers can be cooked by several different methods.

1 JUG METHOD

This minimizes cooking smells: cover the kippers with boiling water, put on a lid or a saucer and leave without further heating for 5 minutes.

2 BOIL IN THE BAG

This minimizes washing up. Boil-in-the-bag kippers merely need to be simmered according to the packet instructions, before being turned out on to the serving plate.

3 GRILLING

For some, the smell of grilling kippers is one of the joys of breakfast; and many think that the best flavour comes when the kipper is grilled under moderately high heat until the backbone is partly charred (about 10 minutes – no need to turn).

For all methods, serve with a wedge of lemon. Also with a thick slice of bread. (This is a precaution: a chunk of bread rapidly swallowed helps to avoid choking on tiny unseen bones!)

Baked French toast

Serves 2

Oven temperature: 230°C, 450°F, gas mark 8

Cooking time: 10 minutes

INGREDIENTS

2 large slices medium-cut white or wholemeal bread
1 egg
4 tablespoons milk
2 or 3 drops vanilla essence (optional)
1 ½–2 oz (45–55 g) cornflakes, finely crushed
1 oz (30 g) butter or margarine, melted

Serve with marmalade or jam *or* wedges of cored dessert apple dipped in clear honey *or* eggs and bacon.

METHOD

1 Cut each slice of bread across in half to form 2 triangles.
2 In a shallow dish, beat the egg with a fork. Stir in the
  milk and vanilla essence.
3 Put the crushed cornflakes on a large plate.
4 Dip each bread triangle into the egg mixture, turning
  once and allowing the bread to absorb the mixture.
5 Coat with the finely crushed cornflakes.
6 Place in a single layer on a well-greased baking tin,
  and trickle a little melted butter over the bread.
7 Bake in a hot oven for about 10 minutes, until lightly
  brown.

Three-fruit marmalade

This is an excellent year-round preserve to make when Seville oranges are out of season.

Makes 5 lb (2.3 kg), prepared over two days

INGREDIENTS

1 grapefruit
2 lemons ⎫ weighing in total about 1 ½–2 lb (0.7–0.9 kg)
1 sweet orange ⎭
glycerine or butter
3 lb (1.4 kg) sugar, granulated or preserving

METHOD

1 Scrub and peel the fruit. If the pith is very thick, remove some of it. With a sharp knife, shred the peel finely or coarsely according to taste.
2 Roughly cut up the fruit, tying the pips, pith and stringy parts in a muslin bag.
3 Put the fruit, peel and muslin bag to soak with 3 pints (1.7 litres) water in a large bowl for 24 hours.
4 Next day, rub the interior of a preserving pan with glycerine or butter to prevent foaming during cooking. Transfer the contents of the bowl to the pan and mark the level with a pencil on an upright wooden spoon.
5 Simmer for 1 ½ hours, or until the peel is tender and the contents of the pan, again measured on the wooden spoon, are reduced by about one third.

6 Remove the muslin bag, after squeezing gently into the pan. (This extracts pectin which helps to set the marmalade.)

7 Add the sugar and stir over a low heat until thoroughly dissolved.

8 Bring to the boil and boil rapidly until setting point is reached (see below).

9 Remove from the heat and leave for 10 minutes for a skin to form. Stir to distribute the peel and pour into warmed pots. Cover with waxed circles and jam-pot covers.

Tests for setting point of marmalade

(a) Temperature with a sugar thermometer reaches about 221°F (105°C). Sometimes a set is reached at a slightly lower or higher temperature, so combine this test with:

(b) Stir with a wooden spoon, and twirl it above the mixture; the marmalade when ready to set will fall off in flakes rather than in drops.

(c) Put a little of the marmalade on a saucer and cool rapidly, preferably in the refrigerator. The marmalade is set when it wrinkles heavily when pushed with your little finger.

Seville orange marmalade (using a processor or liquidizer)

This can be made following the method given for Three-fruit Marmalade. But it is much speedier to use a food processor or a liquidizer to prepare the oranges. This method also does away with the need to soak the cut-up fruit overnight. The peel is not so carefully cut, but the flavour is just as good.

Makes 10 lb (4.5 kg)

INGREDIENTS

3 lb (1.4 kg) Seville oranges
glycerine or butter
juice of 2 lemons
6 lb (2.8 kg) sugar (granulated or preserving)

METHOD

1 Scrub the oranges, removing the stalks. Cut across in halves and then into quarters and eighths, cutting any stringy parts from the middle of the fruit to help you to remove the pips (see illustration).
2 Put the pips and stringy parts in a muslin square placed in a bowl to collect extra juice. Tie the muslin into a loose bag with cotton, leaving the ends long enough to tie on to the pan handle.
3 Grease the preserving pan with glycerine or butter.

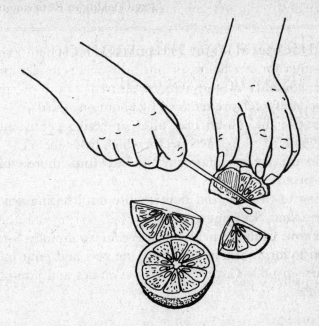

4 *Using food processor*: place some of the cut-up oranges into the bowl of the food processor, fitted with the blade, and process for a few seconds until coarsely chopped. Transfer to the preserving pan. Repeat in batches with the rest of the oranges. Add 6 pints (3.4 litres) water, orange juice from the cutting up, the lemon juice and the muslin bag. Mark the level on a wooden spoon.

Using liquidizer: measure out 6 pints (3.4 litres) water. Half fill the goblet of a liquidizer with cut-up oranges and fill to within an inch or two of the top with water from the measured amount. Process at high speed for a few seconds only, just sufficient to chop the peel coarsely. Pour into the preserving pan. Repeat with the rest of the oranges, adding the rest of the water, the orange juice from the cutting up, the lemon juice and the bag. Mark the level on a wooden spoon.

5 Simmer for 1½ hours, or until the peel is tender and the contents of the pan, measured again on the wooden spoon, are reduced by about one third.

6 Remove the muslin bag, after squeezing gently into the pan. (This extracts pectin which helps the set.)

7 Add the sugar, stir over a low heat until thoroughly dissolved.

8 Bring to the boil and boil rapidly until setting point is reached. See page 219.

9 Remove from the heat and leave for 10 minutes for a skin to form. Stir to distribute the peel and pour into warmed pots. Cover with waxed circles and jam-pot covers.

Evelyn's wholemeal bread

This bread is very easy to make. You will need a 2 lb (1 kg) loaf tin, preferably non-stick.

Oven temperature: 220°C, 425°F gas mark 7 for 10 minutes; reduce heat to 180°C, 350°F, gas mark 4 for a further 15 minutes

INGREDIENTS

4 teaspoons honey *or* black treacle *or* sugar
2 teaspoons active dry yeast
15 oz (425 g) stoneground wholemeal flour
1 teaspoon salt
1 tablespoon sunflower oil

METHOD

1 Add ½ pint (285 ml) tepid water to the honey (or other type of sugar) and yeast. Stir well and set in a warm place until the yeast mixture is frothy.

2 When frothy, add to the flour, salt and oil, and mix well with a wooden spoon.

3 Turn on to a floured board and knead well.

4 Either shape into a round cottage loaf or put in the loaf tin. Cover with a cloth and put in a warm place until the dough has doubled in bulk.

5 Bake at 220°C, 425°F, gas mark 7 for 10 minutes, and then reduce the heat to 180°C, 350°F, gas mark 4 for a further 15 minutes.

The recipe can be varied by changing the flour, using one third plain white flour to two thirds wholemeal.

Or mash up a large, very ripe banana, ripe enough to have a blackened skin, and add it to a honey wholemeal loaf. When it has risen, paint the top with beaten egg and sprinkle it with sesame seeds. This bread toasts beautifully.

Breakfast or brunch ideas from holidays

Some of these breakfasts were eaten abroad at friends' homes. Others were proffered as 'traditional' in hotels.

The lists below – to which I am sure many of you could add – may even give inspiration for a holiday-at-home breakfast or brunch. Most of the items can now be found at local shops and supermarkets in this country.

Canada: bran muffins, pancakes, maple syrup, thin-cut streaky bacon.

Danish brunch: milk, skimmed and full cream, plain yogurt, Ymer (a cultured milk product, similar to smetana), fruit, fruit juices, cereals, boiled eggs, salami, other assorted cold meats, Danish cheeses (Samsø, Danbo, Elbo, Fynbo, Esrom, Havarti), breads (various types of ryebread and white bread), crispbread, rolls, Danish pastries, coffee or tea.

Finland: soured milk and buttermilk, compote of berry fruits.

France: chocolate croissants, small brioches, French sticks, strawberry preserve, hot chocolate.

Israel: fresh orange slices, avocados, olives, pickled herrings, tomatoes, cucumber, radishes, yogurt, cottage cheese, thin-sliced cheeses, boiled eggs, rye and white bread, cakes.

Korea: grilled fish, turnip soup, seaweed, *kimchi* (seasoned and fermented pickle of cabbage, turnip, cucumber and other seasonable vegetables), ginseng tea.

Netherlands: sliced cheeses and ham, eaten together on bread, sweeter bread slices containing juicy sultanas.

Norway: jam with milk on breakfast cereals, marinaded herrings, sliced meats, boiled eggs, glass of milk and a cup of coffee; bread (approximately 30–60 per cent wholemeal flour) with low-fat spread, margarine or butter, and cheese, jam, liver pâté or a fish such as canned mackerel in tomato sauce.

Scotland: oatmeal porridge with salt, Arbroath smokies, Loch Fyne kippers, finnan haddock.

USA: blueberry muffins, waffles with sausages and maple syrup or with strawberries and cream, hash brown potatoes, eggs cooked to your choice, including steak and eggs, or five-egg omelettes (although I settled for the 'side order' of a mere two eggs).

Chapter Seven
Afternoon Teas

Sandwiches
Small bridge rolls
Open sandwiches
Scones (honey and yogurt)
Bran fruit loaf (eggless)
Apple cake
Banana and nut bread (one stage)
Carrot cake with cream-cheese frosting
Cheesecake
Chocolate freezer biscuits (unbaked)
Coconut pyramids
Fruit and nut teabread
Cookie log (unbaked)
Ginger and pineapple tart
Macaroons – almond
Macaroons – chocolate
Shortbread with pine nuts
Victoria sandwich cake (chocolate)
Sponge cake – continental
Sponge cake – Gilly's
Evelyn's coffee and walnut cake

Sandwiches

For afternoon-tea elegance, nothing can beat cucumber sandwiches: thinly sliced and sparingly buttered good-quality white bread sandwiched with peeled, lightly salted, fresh cucumber slices, crusts removed, sandwiches cut into dainty fingers or triangles. With these I impress visitors from abroad!

Other ever-popular fillings: egg mayonnaise, garnished with cress; mashed sardine and tomato; cream cheese and slivers of stem ginger.

Small bridge rolls

Slash the tops of small bridge rolls, butter lightly and insert wedges of tomato, apple dipped in lemon juice, and cheese dipped in chutney. (See illustration on page 229.)

Open sandwiches

Open sandwiches can be left large (crusts left on for easy handling) or served as small canapés, if the bread is first cut into rounds with pastry cutters.

They are best spread with a layer of cream cheese or curd cheese, or chutney or other flavouring, on to which the toppings can be decoratively balanced with crisp small lettuce leaves, radicchio or other salad leaves. For small quantities, search the delicatessen counters for ready-made salads, including coleslaw, and for a variety of cooked meats and fish. Use decorative garnishes such as twisted slices of orange or lemon, sprigs of fresh herbs, halved seeded grapes, stuffed olives or Pickled Prunes (see page 336).

Some popular toppings

Cold roast beef, corned beef or pastrami on a thin spread of horseradish cream or mild mustard, with coleslaw and a fan of gherkin or sweet/sour pickled cucumber;

slices of turkey roll, decorated with endive, and garnished with cranberry sauce;

marinaded herring pieces (or cooked peeled shrimps or smoked salmon pieces) on a spread of curd or cream cheese, small lettuce leaves, asparagus tips, tomato wedges or cucumber slices, orange or lemon twists and dill;

Open sandwich

Small bridge roll
with apple and cheese

Small canapés

Gherkin garnish

Red Leicester cheese, sliced down in triangles, on a spread of peach chutney, decorated with radicchio and segments of cherry tomato;

hard-boiled egg slices, garnished with mayonnaise flavoured with tomato paste and decorated with the dark green small leaves of lambs' lettuce;

cottage cheese topped with a ring of canned pineapple and a ring of red pepper, and garnished with cress and lettuce.

Scones (honey and yogurt)

Makes 8–9 scones

Oven temperature: 200°C, 400°F, gas mark 6

Cooking time: 15–18 minutes

INGREDIENTS

2 oz (55 g) butter or margarine
8 oz (225 g) fine self-raising flour
1 teaspoon baking powder
a small pinch of salt
grated zest of half lemon
2 teaspoons clear honey
small carton (5 fl oz, 140 ml) natural yogurt
2–4 tablespoons milk
a little milk for glazing

METHOD

1 Rub the fat into the flour, baking powder and salt until the mixture resembles fine breadcrumbs. Stir in the lemon zest.
2 Stir in the honey, yogurt and milk, adding just sufficient milk to form a soft dough.
3 Knead lightly on a floured surface until smooth.
4 Roll out to ½ inch (1 cm) thickness and cut into wedges or 2½ inch (6 cm) rounds.
5 Place on a greased baking sheet, brush with milk and bake for 15–18 minutes until well risen and golden brown. Cool on a wire rack. Split and serve with strawberries and cream, or jam and Cornish cream.

Bran fruit loaf (eggless)

Makes about 10–12 slices

Oven temperature: 180°C, 350°F, gas mark 4

Cooking time: approximately 1 hour after a preliminary 30 minutes soaking

You will need a 2 lb (1 kg) loaf tin, well greased and lined on the base.

INGREDIENTS

4 oz (115 g) All-Bran
4 oz (115 g) caster sugar
10 oz (285 g) mixed dried fruit
½ pint (285 ml) milk
4 oz (115 g) self-raising flour

METHOD

1 Put All-Bran, sugar and dried fruit into a bowl and mix them well together. Stir in the milk and leave to stand for 30 minutes to soak.
2 Sieve in the flour, mixing well, and pour the mixture into the prepared loaf tin.
3 Bake in a moderate oven for about an hour, until firm to the touch, browning and coming away from the sides of the tin.
4 Turn out on to a cooling rack.
5 When cold, cut into slices and spread with butter or margarine. Or slice and freeze; toast from frozen.

Apple cake

Can be served fresh, but it also freezes well.

Serves 12

Oven temperature: 180°C, 350°F, gas mark 4

Cooking time: 45 minutes to 1 hour.

You will need a 9 inch (23 cm) square cake tin or a 10 inch (25 cm) round cake tin, greased and lined on the base.

INGREDIENTS

6 oz (170 g) self-raising flour
pinch of salt
½ teaspoon ground cinnamon
½ teaspoon grated nutmeg
1 lb (450 g) cooking apples
4 oz (115 g) butter or margarine
6 oz (170 g) caster sugar
2 eggs, size 3
2 oz (55 g) All-Bran or Bran Buds

Fluffy icing
1 tablespoon plain flour
3 tablespoons milk
2 oz (55 g) softened butter
2 oz (55 g) caster sugar

METHOD

1 Sift together the flour, salt, cinnamon and nutmeg.
2 Peel, core and finely chop the apples.
3 Beat the 4 oz (115 g) butter or margarine and 6 oz (170 g) sugar together until light and fluffy.
4 Beat in the eggs, one at a time, adding a tablespoon of the flour mixture if necessary to prevent curdling.
5 Fold in the rest of the sieved flour, apples and All-Bran or Bran Buds.
6 Turn into the prepared tin, levelling the mixture.
7 Bake in a moderate oven for 45 minutes to 1 hour, until the cake is golden brown and shrinking away from the sides of the tin.
8 Turn on to a cooling rack and leave until cold.

To make the icing
1 Put the flour into a small saucepan and gradually stir in the milk. Cook over a low heat, stirring constantly, until a thick paste forms. Remove from the heat and leave until cold.
2 Beat the butter with the sugar until light and fluffy (for speed, use an electric hand whisk).
3 Add the cooled flour paste and continue to whisk thoroughly until light and of a spreading consistency.
4 Spread over the cake; cut into squares.

To freeze: place the cut-up iced cake on a foil-lined baking tray and freeze uncovered until hard. Wrap separately in freezer film, seal in a polythene bag and return to the freezer. To serve, unwrap while still frozen and allow to thaw at room temperature for about 3 hours.

Banana and nut bread (one stage)

Can be frozen in slices.

Oven temperature: 180°C, 350°F, gas mark 4

Cooking time: 1 ¼ hours

You will need a 2 lb (1 kg) loaf tin, bottom-lined with greaseproof or silicone paper and greased with margarine.

INGREDIENTS

1 egg (size 2)
6 tablespoons milk
3 medium bananas, mashed
grated rind of 1 orange
2 oz (55 g) walnuts, chopped
2 oz (55 g) soft margarine
4 oz (115 g) caster sugar
5 oz (140 g) plain wholemeal flour
5 oz (140 g) plain white flour
1 teaspoon baking powder
¼ teaspoon bicarbonate of soda
½ teaspoon salt

METHOD

1 In a mixing bowl, beat the egg and milk together.
  Add the other ingredients and beat with a wooden
  spoon until well mixed (2–3 minutes).
2 Spoon the mixture (which will be soft) into the
  prepared loaf tin and smooth the top.
3 Bake for about 1¼ hours. Cool on a wire tray. Serve
  sliced and spread with butter or margarine.

Carrot cake with cream-cheese frosting

Serves 8

Conventional cooking
Oven temperature: 180°C, 350°F, gas mark 4
Cooking time: about 65 minutes

For conventional cooking you will need a 2 lb (1 kg) loaf tin, lightly oiled and lined with non-stick baking parchment. If using a non-stick loaf tin, it need only be very lightly oiled and base-lined.

Microwave cooking
Cooking time: 10 minutes on Full power (timing may vary slightly according to the wattage of your microwave). For microwave cooking you will need a 2 lb (1 kg) microwave container, lightly oiled and lined with baking parchment.

INGREDIENTS

4 oz (115 g) dried walnuts
8 oz (225 g) carrots
3 eggs, size 3
1 teaspoon vanilla essence
6 fl oz (170 ml) corn oil
4 oz (115 g) soft brown sugar
6 oz (170 g) wholemeal flour
1 teaspoon baking powder
1 teaspoon ground cinnamon
1 teaspoon salt
1 teaspoon bicarbonate of soda

Cream-cheese frosting
6 oz (170 g) Philadelphia cheese
1 oz (30 g) butter or margarine
½ teaspoon almond essence
8 oz (225 g) icing sugar, sifted

METHOD

1 Chop the walnuts. Peel and grate the carrots.
2 Beat the eggs and vanilla in a mixing bowl. Add the walnuts and carrots and the rest of the ingredients. Beat until well mixed, about 1 minute. (The mixture will be very soft.)

Conventional cooking
3 Spoon into the tin, smoothing the top.
4 Bake until a skewer comes out clean.
5 Allow to cool completely in the tin.
6 Turn out and spread Cream-cheese Frosting over the top and sides.

Microwave cooking
3 Spoon the mixture, prepared as in steps 1 and 2 above, into the microwave container. Hollow the centre.
4 Cook, uncovered, on Full power for 10 minutes. (Timing may vary slightly depending on the wattage of the microwave.)
5 Allow to cool completely in the container.
6 Turn out and spread Cream-cheese Frosting over the sides and top.

To make the cream-cheese frosting
Place all the ingredients in a mixing bowl and beat well with a wooden spoon.

Cheesecake

This cheesecake is served cold.

Serves 8

Oven temperature: 180°C, 350°F, gas mark 4

Cooking time: approximately 30 minutes

You will need a loose-bottomed cake tin or a deep foil flan case approximately 8 inches (20 cm) in diameter.

INGREDIENTS

For biscuit crust
scant 2 oz (50 g) unsalted butter
4 oz (115 g) gingernut biscuits

For filling
2 eggs (size 3), beaten
1 lb (450 g) curd cheese
6 level tablespoons caster sugar

For topping immediately
1 small carton (5 fl oz, 140 ml) soured cream
1 ½ level tablespoons caster sugar

Alternative sauce, for use when the cheesecake has been defrosted
1 small carton (5 fl oz, 140 ml) soured cream
1 ½ tablespoons ginger conserve or ginger marmalade

METHOD

1 Melt the butter in a medium saucepan.
2 Place the biscuits, a few at a time and slightly broken up, in a plastic or paper bag. Crush with a rolling-pin until the consistency of coarse crumbs.*
3 Stir the crumbs into the melted butter.
4 Press into the base of the tin or flan case and allow to cool.
5 Stir the beaten eggs smoothly into the cheese with the 6 level tablespoons sugar.
6 Pour on top of the biscuit crust. Bake for approximately 30 minutes at 180°C, 350°F, gas mark 4.
7 Remove from the oven and *either*
(a) pour on the soured cream lightly beaten with the 1½ level tablespoons sugar and return to the oven for 10 minutes and allow to cool before serving, *or*
(b) cool without adding soured cream and then freeze. To serve, thaw for a few hours and accompany with a sauce of soured cream beaten lightly with ginger conserve or ginger marmalade.

* The biscuits can be crushed in a blender or food processor, gradually adding the melted butter when they have reached the right consistency.

Chocolate freezer biscuits (unbaked)

Makes about 40 biscuits. This is an ideal have-on-hand recipe for unexpected guests. It needs no further cooking, and is ready to eat within moments of removing from the freezer. Slice off what you need and return the rest to the freezer.

INGREDIENTS

18 oz (500 g) digestive biscuits
7 fl oz (200 ml) milk
6 tablespoons cocoa powder
8 oz (225 g) sugar
4 oz (115 g) packet margarine
3 oz (85 g) sultanas

METHOD

1 Break up the biscuits into small pieces.
2 Boil the milk with the cocoa and sugar, add the margarine and allow it to melt.
3 Remove from the heat and stir in the sultanas and broken biscuits. Mix well together. Cool.
4 Form into two long rolls, about 2 inches (5 cm) in diameter, wrap in lightly oiled foil, and put in the freezer.
5 Remove just before needed and cut into slices.

Coconut pyramids

Makes 10–11, or make double quantities for a party

Oven temperature: 150°C, 300°F, gas mark 2

Cooking time: about 20 minutes

You will need sheets of rice paper or silicone paper.

INGREDIENTS

4 oz (115 g) fine-cut desiccated coconut
2½ oz (70 g) caster sugar
1 egg (size 3), beaten
glacé cherries (red, or a mixture of red, yellow and green)
pink colouring (optional)

METHOD

1 Line a baking sheet with the rice paper (which is edible) or silicone paper, which prevents sticking.
2 Mix the coconut and sugar together and fork in sufficient beaten egg to make a slightly moist mixture.
3 Moisten hands with cold water and shape all or half (see step 5) of the mixture into cones or pyramids, using about a tablespoon for each.
4 Place on the baking sheet and top each pyramid with a small piece of glacé cherry.
5 If you wish, stir one or two drops of pink colouring into the second half of the mixture and stir well, so that some of the pyramids are coloured pink.
6 Bake until very lightly browned.
7 Cool before breaking off the surplus rice paper.

Fruit and nut teabread

Makes 10 slices

Oven temperature: 180°C, 350°F, gas mark 4

Cooking time: 1½ hours, after preliminary soaking

You will need a 2 lb (1 kg) loaf tin, well greased and
lined on the base; also some greaseproof paper and foil
to prevent over-browning.

INGREDIENTS

4 oz (115 g) All-Bran
3 oz (85 g) sultanas
3 oz (85 g) raisins
3 oz (85 g) chopped stoneless dates
3 oz (85 g) chopped dried walnuts
1 oz (30 g) chopped hazelnuts
3 oz (85 g) demerara sugar
8 fl oz (225 ml) semi-skimmed milk
5 fl oz (140 ml) natural yogurt
6 oz (170 g) wholemeal self-raising flour

METHOD

1 In a bowl mix the All-Bran, fruits, nuts and sugar.
2 Blend together the milk and yogurt. Pour over the
  bran mixture and leave for at least half an hour.
3 Stir in the flour.
4 Pour into the tin and bake for ½ hour.

5 At the end of the ½ hour cover the top with grease-proof paper, held down by foil, to prevent over-browning. Return to the oven and continue cooking for another hour.

6 Turn out on to a cooling rack.

Store some slices in the freezer for an 'unexpected visitors' stand-by. Wrap up in packets, each containing 4–6 slices separated by greaseproof paper or freezer interleaf wrap. Seal them in kitchen foil or a freezer bag, and label with the amount and date. When visitors arrive, take out the appropriate number of slices and toast from frozen.

Cookie log (unbaked)

INGREDIENTS

½ pint (285 ml) carton whipping cream
1 packet (9 oz, 255 g) chocolate-chip cookies
a few tablespoons medium-sweet sherry
to decorate: plain chocolate, grated

METHOD

1 Whip the cream stiffly.
2 Quickly dip two biscuits in and out of a shallow plate of sherry so that they soak up some of the flavour without becoming soggy.
3 Join them together with a small blob of whipped cream and stand them upright on the serving platter.
4 Continue to assemble the dipped biscuits, one at a time, with small blobs of cream until they are all used up, forming a 'log' on the serving platter.
5 With a palette knife, cover the log with the rest of the cream. Place in the refrigerator for a few hours so that the biscuits have time to soften.
6 Decorate with grated chocolate before serving.

Ginger and pineapple tart

This needs no cooking. It is best eaten the day it is made, otherwise the pineapple mixture may 'weep'.

INGREDIENTS

6 oz (170 g) ginger biscuits (crushed)
2 ½ oz (70 g) softened butter or soft margarine
3 tablespoons ginger marmalade or conserve
¼ pint (140 ml) whipping cream
1 medium can crushed pineapple (drained)

You will need a 9 inch (23 cm) shallow dish or a cake tin with a removable base.

METHOD

1 Mix the biscuit crumbs and butter or margarine and use to line the bottom of the tin.
2 Spread with the ginger marmalade or conserve.
3 Stiffly whip the cream, fold in the well-drained pine-apple and pile on top of the biscuit crust.
4 Refrigerate for an hour or so until needed, and cut in wedges like a cake.

Macaroons – almond

Makes 20

Oven temperature: 190°C, 375°F, gas mark 5

Cooking time: 15–18 minutes

You will need a baking sheet lined with rice paper or silicone paper; the rice paper is edible.

INGREDIENTS

3 egg whites
8 oz (225 g) ground almonds
7 oz (200 g) caster sugar
flaked almonds

METHOD

1 Beat the egg whites until frothy, not stiff. Add ½ tablespoon cold water.
2 Stir gradually into the ground almonds and sugar, using sufficient to make a soft mixture, but firm enough to shape.
3 With moistened hands make small balls of the mixture and put slightly apart on the lined tin, flattened lightly with a fork. Press a flaked almond on top.
4 Bake for about 15–18 minutes until lightly golden but still slightly soft to the touch.
5 Remove from the tin and leave to cool before breaking off the rice paper.

Macaroons – chocolate

Makes 12–15

Oven temperature: 180°C, 350°F, gas mark 4

Cooking time: 15–20 minutes

You will need a baking sheet lined with rice paper or silicone paper; rice paper is edible.

INGREDIENTS

4 oz (115 g) ground almonds
2 oz (55 g) plain chocolate, grated
3½ oz (100 g) caster sugar
½ teaspoon cinnamon
whites of 2 eggs, size 3 or 4

METHOD

1 Mix together the almonds, chocolate, sugar and cinnamon.
2 Beat the egg whites to a soft froth and stir gradually and lightly into the dry ingredients, using sufficient to make a soft mixture, but firm enough to shape.
3 Heap tablespoons of the mixture well apart on the lined tin and bake until firm to the touch, approximately 15–20 minutes.
4 Leave to cool before breaking off the surplus rice paper.

Shortbread with pine nuts

Makes 12 wedges

Oven temperature: 190°C, 375°F, gas mark 5

Cooking time: 30 minutes

INGREDIENTS

6 oz (170 g) plain flour
½ teaspoon ground cinnamon
4 oz (115 g) butter
4 oz (115 g) golden granulated sugar
1 dessertspoon pine nuts
1 teaspoon demerara sugar

You will need a 9 inch (23 cm) diameter shallow tin, preferably with an integral cutting knife that assists turning out.

METHOD

1 Rub together the flour, cinnamon and butter. Stir in the golden sugar and gather together into a ball.*
2 Press smoothly into the tin and mark into 12 wedge-shaped slices.
3 Press on the pine nuts evenly to decorate, and sprinkle with the demerara sugar.
4 Bake for about 30 minutes (it should be beginning to brown, but still soft to the touch). When cool cut into the already marked slices.

* For speed the ingredients can be mixed together in an electric mixer or food processor.

Victoria sandwich cake (chocolate)

Oven temperature: 180°C, 350°F, gas mark 4

Cooking time: 20–25 minutes

Note: if you prefer to mix these cakes by hand, omit the baking powder and bake at 190°C, 375°F, gas mark 5 for approximately 20 minutes. See step-by-step method on page 256.

You will need 2 sponge tins, 7 inches (18 cm) in diameter. Grease them well, fit the base with a circle of cooking parchment and then coat with flour, shaking out excess.

INGREDIENTS

4 oz (115 g) soft margarine or thoroughly softened butter
4 oz (115 g) caster sugar
4 oz (115 g) self-raising flour (**minus 3 level tablespoons**)
1 level teaspoon baking powder (omit if mixing by hand)
3 level tablespoons cocoa*
2 large eggs (size 2)

(*Continued overleaf.*)

* For a moister cake, mix the cocoa to a thick paste with very little warm water or strong coffee before adding to the ingredients.

METHOD

1 Place all ingredients into the bowl of the food processor, fitted with the blade.

2 Process at maximum speed for about 10 seconds, stopping the machine to scrape down after 5 seconds. It should be well creamed but not runny.

3 Transfer to the prepared sponge tins and bake at 180°C, 350°F, gas mark 4 (if mixing by hand, bake at 190°C, 375°F, gas mark 5) until risen, firm to the touch and coming away from the sides of the tin (20–25 minutes).

4 Cool, turn out and sandwich together with your chosen filling. (See opposite.)

5 Decorate by placing a paper doily on top and sieving icing sugar over the surface. Remove the doily to reveal the pattern.

Chocolate butter-cream filling

INGREDIENTS

¾ tablespoon cocoa
2 oz (55 g) butter or margarine
4 oz (115 g) icing sugar

METHOD

Dissolve the cocoa in 1 tablespoon warm water and leave to cool. Cream the butter or margarine until soft. Beat in the icing sugar and the cocoa.

Chocolate peppermint yogurt filling

A quick alternative to the chocolate butter-cream for sandwiching the cakes together.

INGREDIENTS

6 After Eight chocolate peppermints
3–4 tablespoons Greek-style yogurt

METHOD

1 Melt the chocolates in a bowl placed over a pan of hot water.
2 Mix thoroughly with the yogurt and leave in the refrigerator until it thickens slightly.

Sponge cake – continental

Oven temperature: 190°C, 375°F, gas mark 5

Cooking time: 25–30 minutes for 2 small cakes; 40 minutes for 1 larger cake

This mixture makes 2 small cakes (1 × 6–7 inch, 15–18 cm cake tin and 1 ring cake tin) *or* 1 larger cake (8½ inch, 22 cm cake tin). Grease and flour the tins; for preference, use non-stick tins, lightly greased.

INGREDIENTS

4 eggs (size 3)
5 oz (140 g) caster sugar
2½ oz (70 g) plain flour
2½ oz (70 g) potato flour
2 teaspoons baking powder
a small carton (5 fl oz, 140 ml) double or whipping cream
small can (11 oz, 310 g) mandarin oranges or sliced peaches
a little icing sugar for large cake

METHOD

1 Thoroughly whisk together the eggs and sugar until light and foamy.
2 Gently fold in the sifted flours and baking powder.
3 Transfer to the prepared tins and bake, timing according to size, as above.
4 Turn out and cool on a wire rack.

5 When cold, the *smaller cakes* should be filled with a mixture of whipped cream and drained fruit.

The *larger cake* should be cut across to make three layers; drizzle a little of the fruit syrup on to the bottom layer to moisten but avoid making it soggy, then add a layer of fruit; add the second layer, drizzle a little more fruit syrup on top and spread with a thick layer of whipped cream; place the third layer on top and dust with sifted icing sugar.

Sponge cake – Gilly's

This is best made with a hand-held or stand electric mixer.

Serves 8

Oven temperature: 200°C, 400°F, gas mark 6

Cooking time: about 15 minutes for two sponge sandwiches or sponge flans; about 30 minutes for one large sponge

You will need two 8 inch (20 cm) sandwich tins or sponge flan tins. If you want one large sponge cake, use an 8 inch (20 cm) loose-bottom or non-stick cake tin. You can use silicone circles for lining the base of the cake tins.

INGREDIENTS

3 large eggs (size 2)
6 oz (170 g) caster sugar
4 oz (115 g) self-raising flour
jam *and /or* raspberries or strawberries tossed in sugar
whipping cream (for sandwich cake) *or* pouring cream (for large cake)
icing sugar

METHOD

1 Grease and flour the tins. For ease of removal use silicone parchment to line the base of the cake tins.

2 Whisk the eggs and sugar at high speed for at least 5 minutes, until light and foaming.

3 By hand, gradually and lightly sift in and fold in the flour.

4 Pour into the prepared tins and bake on the centre shelf of the oven until well risen, golden and just coming away from the side of the tin. They are done when gentle pressure by the finger results in a dent which begins to return to shape again.

5 Turn out on to cake racks to cool.

6 Sandwich together with whipped cream and jam or fruit. Sift a little icing sugar over the top. Or decorate the top of the large cake with jam and fruit and serve with pouring cream.

The cakes can be frozen separately before filling.
Allow 2 to 3 hours to thaw out at room temperature and then fill or decorate as described.

Evelyn's coffee and walnut cake

Oven temperature: 190°C, 375°F, gas mark 5

Cooking time: 20–25 minutes if baked in two 7 inch (18 cm) sandwich tins, 40–45 minutes if baked in an 8 inch (20 cm) deep tin. Grease and flour the tins. For ease of removal use silicone parchment to line the base.

INGREDIENTS

4 oz (115 g) soft margarine
4 oz (115 g) caster sugar
2 eggs (size 3)
1 tablespoon coffee essence
4 oz (115 g) self-raising flour
2 oz (55 g) chopped walnuts

METHOD

1 Cream the margarine and sugar.
2 Add the eggs one at a time, beating well and adding a tablespoon of the flour to help prevent curdling.
3 Mix in the coffee essence.
4 Sieve the flour and fold in with the chopped walnuts.
5 Transfer to the prepared baking tin(s) and bake until well risen, just firm to the touch, and beginning to come away from the sides of the tin.

Filling for coffee and walnut sandwich cake

2 oz (55 g) soft margarine
4 oz (115 g) sieved icing sugar
2 teaspoons coffee essence
1 teaspoon milk
1 oz (30 g) finely chopped walnuts

METHOD

Cream the margarine and beat in the remaining ingredients.

Coffee glacé icing for top of larger cake

4 oz (115 g) sieved icing sugar
1 teaspoon coffee essence

METHOD

Gradually add the coffee essence and 2 teaspoons warm water to the icing to make it thick enough to coat the back of a spoon. If necessary, add a little more icing sugar or liquid for the desired consistency.

Chapter Eight
Easy Entertaining

SOUPS

Avocado and green pepper (cold)
Broccoli or courgette (microwave)
Jerusalem artichoke
Spinach and pea (store-cupboard)
Stilton and watercress
Tomato, French style

APPETIZERS AND A DRINK

Cheese and chutney dip
   other cocktail snacks
Crudités
Easy dips
Marinaded kippers
Stuffed celery
Non-alcoholic punch

STARTERS

Avocado, orange and grapefruit
Baked eggs with prawns and sweetcorn
Fresh herring pâté
Twice-baked cheese soufflés

VEGETABLES

Beetroot and orange
Braised fennel
Courgette bake
Mixed steamed vegetables with herb butter
Sliced roast potatoes
Pilaf with nuts

SALADS

Crisp green salad
Monty's coleslaw

SAUCES

Microwave hollandaise sauce
Mustard hollandaise sauce

FISH

Baked salmon and spinach
Baked trout and orange
Chinese fish
Four-fish bake

POULTRY

Chicken breast stuffed with mango or kiwi fruit
Honey mustard chicken
Lemon and orange chicken
Sherried turkey with lemons
Poussin with Stilton and port
Roast duckling with citrus gravy
   with apple and onion sauce

MEAT

Beef and raisin meatballs in lemon sauce
Creamed pork
Fillet steak with cream and brandy
Sweet and savoury minced beef
Herb-roasted lamb

DESSERTS

Almond pudding
Banana pudding
Brandy butter (spiced)
Brûlée creams (uncooked)
Cherry frangipane flan
Cherries jubilee
Peaches, stuffed and baked
Gilly's sweet pastry
Melon and grape dessert
Pears in blackberry sauce
Raspberry dessert (chilled)

FRUIT AND CHEESE

Cheese and fruit kebabs
Mini-fruits platter
Plated fruit salad

FRUIT PRESERVES

Bacchanalian dried-fruit salad
Preserved orange slices
Pickled prunes

Avocado and green pepper soup (cold)

For this recipe you need either a food processor or a blender or liquidizer.

Serves 2

INGREDIENTS

1 large ripe avocado
1 medium green pepper
½ dessertspoon lemon juice
salt and pepper
½ pint (285 ml) cold milk
2 tablespoons natural yogurt

METHOD

1 Halve, stone and peel the avocado. With a sharp knife, thinly peel the green pepper, halve and de-seed.
2 In a blender,* liquidize the avocado, green pepper, lemon juice, seasonings and cold milk to make a smooth purée. Taste for lemon flavouring and seasoning.
3 Stir in a swirl of yogurt and serve cold.

---

* If using a food processor, purée the ingredients together before mixing in the cold milk.

Broccoli or courgette soup (microwave)

This is a lower-calorie version of creamed soups.

Serves 6

Timing may vary slightly depending on the wattage of the microwave, and the vegetable used. At step 1 test after 3½ minutes. At step 3, courgettes may be fork tender after 10 minutes.

It can be prepared ahead and re-heated for serving later. To re-heat, stir through several times, cover and cook on Medium High (400–500 watts) stirring once or twice until heated through.

INGREDIENTS

2 oz (55 g) butter or margarine
1 medium onion chopped
1¾ pt (1 litre) hot chicken stock
1½ lb (¾ kg) broccoli (or courgettes)
8 fl oz (225 ml) semi-skimmed milk
½ teaspoon salt
⅛ teaspoon white pepper

METHOD

1 Combine the butter and onion in a 3 quart (3½ litre) casserole. Cover and cook on High (600–700 watts) for 3½–5 minutes, stirring once.
2 Stir in the heated stock.

3 Trim and cut the broccoli into florets plus slices of
  stem. *Or* slice the unpeeled courgettes. Stir into the
  stock, cover and continue to cook on High for 10–15
  minutes, stirring twice. Test with a fork for tenderness.
4 Stir the milk into the soup. Cover and continue to
  cook on High for 2 minutes. Let it stand covered for
  5 minutes.
5 Season and taste for flavour.
6 Transfer to a blender or food processor in batches to
  purée.

Jerusalem artichoke soup

Nowadays it is sometimes possible to find large, smooth Jerusalem artichokes in the shops. These are far less trouble to peel than the small knobbly variety, so I look for them when I want to make this delicious soup.

Serves 2

INGREDIENTS

1 lb (450 g) Jerusalem artichokes
juice from ½ lemon
1 small leek
1 oz (30 g) butter
1 pint (565 ml) light chicken stock
salt and pepper
a few chopped chives or sprigs of parsley to garnish

METHOD

1 Peel the artichokes thinly (easiest with a potato peeler). Slice roughly and drop into a pan of cold water, acidulated with the lemon juice. This prevents discoloration.
2 Clean the leek, discarding the tough green top, and slice thinly.
3 Drain the artichokes and fry very gently with the leek in the melted butter. Continue to cook, stirring to avoid browning, for 15 minutes.
4 Add the stock and seasoning. Cover and simmer for about 20 minutes until the vegetables are tender.
5 Sieve, or purée in a liquidizer or processor.
6 Reheat gently and garnish before serving.

Spinach and pea soup (store-cupboard)

Keep these ingredients in the cupboard to serve a speedy soup for unexpected guests.

Serves 2–3

INGREDIENTS

can (14 oz, 400 g) chopped spinach
can (19½ oz, 550 g) garden peas
1 teaspoon dried mint
2 teaspoons dried onion
½ pint (285 ml) milk (can be longlife or reconstituted from milk powder)
black pepper and nutmeg

METHOD

1 Simmer the spinach and peas, plus the liquor from the cans, with the mint, onion and ¼ pint (140 ml) water for 10 minutes; this should give time for the onion to soften.
2 Liquidize to a smooth purée.
3 Heat the milk to steaming point, just below boiling.
4 Stir the purée into the milk and taste for seasoning.

Stilton and watercress soup

This soup can be frozen after step 6 and gently reheated without boiling.

Serves 6

INGREDIENTS

1 medium onion
2 sticks celery
1 bunch watercress
2 tablespoons butter
1 ½ tablespoons flour
1 ½ pints (850 ml) chicken stock
¼ cup white Martini, Cinzano or white wine
½ pint (285 ml) milk
6 oz (170 g) blue Stilton cheese
seasoning
3 tablespoons natural yogurt

METHOD

1 Chop the onion, celery and watercress, and sauté lightly to soften in the butter.
2 Stir in the flour and cook gently for a minute or two.
3 Remove from the heat and gradually stir in the stock and wine. Bring to the boil, stirring. Simmer for 40 minutes.
4 Add the milk and cheese slowly. Allow the cheese to melt and heat, but do not boil.
5 Purée in a blender or food processor.
6 Season to taste with pepper, and salt if needed.
7 Serve hot, with a spoonful of yogurt in each bowl.

Tomato soup, French style

Serves 4–5

INGREDIENTS

2 slices smoked bacon, chopped
1 tablespoon butter
2 large onions, finely sliced
4–6 ripe tomatoes, peeled and de-seeded *or* a can (14 oz,
    400 g) peeled tomatoes
1 tablespoon tomato purée
2 strips lemon rind, peeled thinly
1 ¾ pints (1 litre) chicken stock
salt and pepper
1 teaspoon sugar
1 tablespoon fresh parsley, chopped
¼ teaspoon fresh basil, chopped
for garnish: an extra 1 tablespoon mixed chopped parsley
    and basil, fried garlic croûtons

METHOD

1 Heat bacon in a saucepan. When the fat has run, add butter and when melted add the onions and cook gently until tender and turning golden.
2 Add tomatoes, tomato purée, lemon rind, stock, salt and pepper, sugar and herbs and bring to the boil.
3 Simmer for 20 minutes until the tomatoes are tender.
4 If you like a lemony tang, leave the lemon rind in, otherwise discard it. Put the pan contents through a food mill, or blend in an electric blender. Adjust seasonings. Serve hot, sprinkled with herbs and croûtons.

Cheese and chutney dip

This is a short-cut method, to save serving time.

INGREDIENTS

fruit chutney, e.g. peach
cubes of cheese, e.g. Red Leicester, Double Gloucester
seedless grapes, pineapple pieces

METHOD

1 Spread the serving dishes with a thick layer of fruit chutney.
2 Spear a piece of fruit, followed by a cube of cheese, on to cocktail sticks and stand them upright, with the cheese dipping into the chutney, ready to serve.

Variations

Many delicatessens sell small ready-prepared cocktail snacks, or you may prefer to prepare your own. Skewer them on to cocktail sticks and stand them upright in the appropriate relish, spread thickly on a platter for ease of serving. Here are a few examples:

In mango chutney
cocktail sausages
tiny meat balls

In tartare sauce
tiny fish balls
garlic mushrooms

In a thick tomato relish
king prawns
small vegetarian rissoles
chicken nuggets

Crudités

This starter is especially useful if you plan to follow it with a one-dish main course (e.g. pasta) without cooked vegetables.

Arrange washed vegetables attractively in a decorative basket or bowl. Do not over-prepare: encourage your guests to slice off what they need and to help themselves. The selection may include unpeeled cucumber (some shops sell small whole cucumbers), cherry tomatoes (red or yellow), large green, orange, red or yellow peppers, wiped button mushrooms, chicory, small peeled carrots, celery hearts, radishes, cauliflower florets.

Offer with bowls of flavoured mayonnaise (see next recipe) or French dressing, e.g. oil and vinegar dressing flavoured with honey.

Alternative

Follow the French custom of serving a green salad as a separate course *before* the main meal. The ingredients can be prepared ahead and kept crisp and fresh in the refrigerator.

Serve either in a large bowl or on individual salad plates. Use simple mixtures of salad leaves, garnished with croûtons or olives and tossed in a vinaigrette dressing just before serving.

Easy dips

Prepare sticks of assorted raw vegetables, e.g. carrot, celery, courgette, red, yellow and green peppers, baby sweetcorn and florets of cauliflower. Arrange these round a selection of dips.

The dips

Equal quantities of mayonnaise and fromage frais, flavoured with:

grated apple and curry paste

curry paste and chutney sauce, or the runny part of the chutney

tomato ketchup, tomato purée and a few drops of tabasco sauce

a good-quality whole-grain mustard, e.g. one already mixed with wine, or mustard powder made up with port.

These dips are also suitable for arranging on the table around a meat fondue or for using in place of plain mayonnaise as a dressing for salads.

Marinaded kippers

Prepare this at least two days before it is to be eaten.

INGREDIENTS

1 kipper fillet
juice of 1–2 lemons *or* 2–4 tablespoons bottled lemon juice
¼ teaspoon whole-grain or Dijon mustard
approximately 1 tablespoon caster sugar
freshly ground black pepper

METHOD

1 Cut the kipper fillet lengthways in half and pull off the skin.
2 Cut into diagonal slices about ½–¾ inch (1½–2 cm) wide.
3 In a glass dish, fork the lemon juice, mustard and sugar together, beginning with the smaller quantity of lemon juice and then tasting for desired sharpness or sweetness.
4 Lay the raw kipper slices in this marinade, basting with the liquor, and seasoning with a few grinds of pepper. Cover and refrigerate.
5 Turn once or twice a day before serving, speared on cocktail sticks, as an appetizer.

Marinaded kippers can also be cut up and used as a garnish, on canapés, in cottage-cheese sandwiches or on scrambled egg.

Stuffed celery

I well remember mashing cream cheese with single cream and then piping it into washed and dried celery sticks to make celery bites. I no longer bother with the piping bag and nozzle and have substituted Gorgonzola cheese and port in the following recipe.

Makes approximately 12 'bites'

INGREDIENTS

1 ½ oz (45 g) Gorgonzola cheese
1 tablespoon plain yogurt
1 teaspoon port
2 large sticks tender celery
paprika, olives or black grapes for garnish

METHOD

1 Mash the cheese with the yogurt and port, and fork into the celery sticks.
2 Cut each stick into pieces approximately 1 ½ inches (4 cm) long.
3 Sprinkle the centre with paprika and garnish the plate with olives or halved and pipped black grapes.

Non-alcoholic punch

For those cutting down on alcohol you can serve
Spritzer: a refreshing mixture of white wine and soda
water; or buy low-alcohol drinks. For non-drinkers or
those who sensibly refuse to drink and drive, serve this
well-chilled non-alcoholic punch.

INGREDIENTS

cartons of mixed fruit juices (preferably a carton including
   about 5 different juices)
ginger ale (low-calorie if you wish)
optional: small slices of unpeeled apple and sprigs of borage
   for decoration

**Proportions: allow 1 litre fruit juice to every 2
litres of ginger ale**.

METHOD

1 Mix the fruit juices with the ginger ale in a large jug,
  ready for pouring into glasses. If you prefer to use a
  punch bowl, decorate with the apple or other sliced
  fruit and borage.
2 Chill or serve with ice cubes.

Avocado, orange and grapefruit

Serves 4 as a starter or dessert

INGREDIENTS

1 large orange
1 grapefruit (preferably pink)
1 ripe avocado

For starter
oil and vinegar dressing
chopped parsley for garnish

For dessert
fromage frais
clear honey
cocktail cherries for garnish

METHOD

1 If it is to be served as a starter, grate a little of the orange rind; peel the orange and grapefruit and cut into long, membrane-free segments.
2 Halve, stone and peel the avocado and cut the flesh into segments, dipping briefly in the citrus juices to prevent discoloration.
3 Arrange the three fruits in a fan or circle on the plate.

4 *For a starter*: drizzle with oil and vinegar dressing sharpened with orange zest. Garnish with chopped parsley.
For a dessert: mix fromage frais with the fruit juices and sweeten with clear honey. Drizzle over the fruits. Garnish with cocktail cherries.

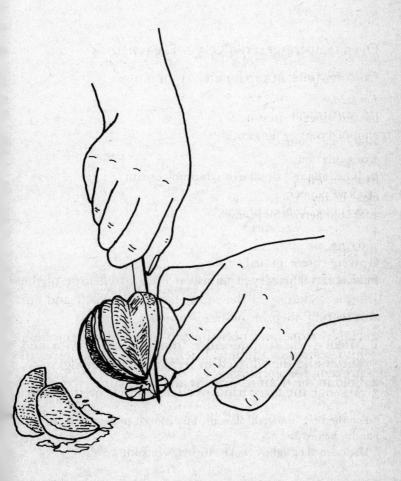

Baked eggs with prawns and sweetcorn

The prawn and sweetcorn sauce can be prepared ahead and refrigerated.

Serves 4–6

Oven temperature: 180°C, 350°F, gas mark 4

Cooking time: approximately 15 minutes

INGREDIENTS

1 oz (30 g) flour
1 oz (30 g) butter
½ pint (285 ml) double or whipping cream
salt and pepper
4 oz (115 g) cooked prawns*
4 oz (115 g) sweetcorn†
4–6 eggs, size 4
Gruyère cheese, grated
small sprigs of parsley to garnish

METHOD

1　Make a thick white sauce from a roux of flour and butter and the whisked-in cream and seasonings.
2　Fold in the drained prawns and sweetcorn.

* For the best 'sea-fresh' flavour, buy cooked prawns in brine and pat dry before use.
† Use canned or lightly cooked frozen sweetcorn.

3 Keep cold in the refrigerator.
4 Spoon 2–3 tablespoons of the mixture into small ovenproof sauté dishes. Make a well in the centre, drop a whole egg into each and season lightly.
5 Sprinkle with grated cheese and bake until the egg is set (approximately 15 minutes). Garnish with a sprig of parsley.

Note: if you are using cast-iron sauté pans, instead of using the oven, reheat the sauce on top of the stove and finish the dish quickly under the grill.

Fresh herring pâté

This was my mother-in-law's recipe; she used a mincer, but I find it simpler nowadays to use a food processor, which makes a fairly coarse pâté.

INGREDIENTS

1 large or 2 small fresh herrings*
1 rollmop
1 apple (preferably Cox's Orange Pippin), peeled and cored
1 small onion, sliced
2 hard-boiled eggs
1 slice stale bread (if mincing) or 1 digestive biscuit
2–3 dessertspoons lemon juice or vinegar
sugar to taste
pepper and salt

Serve with toast, crackers or water biscuits.

METHOD

1 Grill the herrings or bake in foil or use a microwave. Flake the flesh from the skin and bones (you can ignore the very small, very fine bones).
2 Put the fresh herrings and the skinned rollmop through the coarse blade of a mincer, or into the food processor, together with the apple, onion and 1 shelled hard-boiled egg.

* If possible, ask the fishmonger to fillet the herrings.

3 Clean out the mincer with dry bread, allowing a little of the bread to mix into the herring pâté. An alternative when using a food processor: blend with a digestive biscuit.

4 Moisten and flavour to taste with the lemon juice or vinegar, sugar and seasonings.

5 Decorate with slices of hard-boiled egg.

Twice-baked cheese soufflés

Forget the terrors of serving soufflés to unpunctual
guests: these are baked the day (or several days) before,
and are merely reheated!

Serves 6 as a first course

Oven temperature: 180°C, 350°F, gas mark 4

Cooking time: 20 minutes for the first baking, plus 10
minutes for the second baking

You will need
6 × 3 inch (7 cm) ramekins, generously brushed with
    melted butter
6 individual small ovenproof dishes
a roasting pan for a bain-marie (optional)

INGREDIENTS

¼ pint (140 ml) milk
2 level tablespoons flour
1 oz (30 g) butter
shake of pepper
large pinch of mustard
3 oz (85 g) grated mature Cheddar cheese
2 egg yolks (from size 4 eggs)*
4 egg whites (from size 4 eggs)

* The two left-over egg yolks could be used in Courgette Bake (page
285).

For the second baking
¼ pint (140 ml) double cream
grated Parmesan cheese
1 tomato, peeled, seeded and diced (optional)

METHOD

1 Make a thick white sauce with the milk, flour and butter; season with pepper and mustard. (Salt is not needed because cheese is to be added.)

2 Remove from the heat and beat in the Cheddar cheese to melt. Taste again for seasoning.

3 Separate the eggs and add 2 of the yolks to the sauce one at a time, beating well.

4 Whisk the 4 egg whites fairly stiffly (a little stiffer than the cheese mixture).

5 Loosen the cheese mixture by stirring in a couple of tablespoons of the beaten egg whites, then lightly fold the cheese mixture into the rest of the whites.

6 Pour into the ramekins, leaving room for the mixture to rise.

7 Bake in the oven for about 20 minutes until risen and golden brown. **For a more even rise you may prefer to stand the ramekins in a roasting pan half-filled with warm water when baking**.

8 Cool the cooked soufflés: they will fall as they cool but do not worry, they will remain light in texture. When cold, keep in the ramekins in the refrigerator. (They can be kept refrigerated for several days.)

(*Continued overleaf.*)

For the second baking

1 Preheat the oven to 180°C, 350°F, gas mark 4.
2 Carefully turn out the cold soufflés on to individual small ovenproof dishes.
3 When your guests have arrived, pour double cream over and around the soufflés, sprinkle the top with the grated Parmesan and, if you want extra colour, add a few pieces of diced tomato to the cream.
4 Bake in the preheated oven for about 10 minutes. Serve hot, placing the oven dishes on serving plates to help to protect the table from the heat of the dishes.

Beetroot and orange

Try this served with meatcakes, fishcakes or vegeburgers. Serve hot or cold.

Serves 2 (for 4 servings, double the quantity of beetroot, but use the same amount of orange sauce)

INGREDIENTS

½ lb (225 g) cooked small beetroot (not pickled)
2–3 medium oranges
½ tablespoon demerara sugar
salt and black pepper
½ tablespoon cornflour

METHOD

1 Slice the peeled beetroot.
2 Cut a few slivers of zest from the oranges (the outer rind without the pith). Slice into small, thin matchsticks.
3 Juice the oranges (about ¼ pint, 140 ml) and place in a small pan with the sliced orange zest, 3 tablespoons cold water, sugar and seasonings. Bring to the boil, stirring to dissolve the sugar.
4 Mix the cornflour with a little water to a smooth runny paste, stir in some of the orange syrup and return to the pan, still stirring to thicken.
5 Add the beetroot and simmer gently until thoroughly warmed.

Braised fennel

This can be cooked on top of the stove or in a moderate oven.

Serves 1–2

Cooking time: approximately 1 hour

INGREDIENTS

1–2 heads of fennel
a knob of butter
⅓ pint (200 ml) hot vegetable stock (or stock made with a
   piece of chicken cube)
2 teaspoons lemon juice
salt and black pepper
1 teaspoon butter
1 teaspoon flour

METHOD

1 Cut the fennel in half lengthwise after trimming off
   the roots, tops and the outer leaves if tough.*
2 Place the fennel in a small casserole, dot with pieces
   of butter and pour on the stock, lemon juice and seasoning.
3 Cover and simmer slowly for an hour or until tender.
4 Cream the teaspoon of butter and flour into a paste
   and stir into the hot juices until thickened.

* If you are not fond of a dominant aniseed flavour, cover with
cold water, bring to the boil, simmer for 20 minutes, then pour off
the water and continue from step 2. Cooking time at step 3 will
then be halved.

Courgette bake

Courgette Bake can be served as a vegetable, or with Greek yogurt and potatoes as a vegetarian main course.

It can be served hot immediately it is cooked, or cooled and then reheated later or next day.

Serves 4

Oven temperature: 190°C, 375°F, gas mark 5

Cooking time: approximately 40 minutes

INGREDIENTS

1–1 ½ lb (0.7 kg) courgettes
dried minced garlic
salt and black pepper
dried thyme *or* chopped fresh coriander
2–3 oz (55–85 g) Cheddar or Gruyère cheese, grated
2 eggs *or* 3 egg yolks
½ pint (285 ml) full-cream milk or whipping cream

METHOD

1 Coarsely grate the unpeeled courgettes and mix in an ovenproof dish with the garlic, seasoning and herbs.
2 Scatter with a layer of cheese.
3 Lightly whisk the eggs, beat into the milk or cream and pour into the casserole. Stir thoroughly.
4 Bake uncovered for approximately 40 minutes, until the top is golden. It will be slightly liquid.

Mixed steamed vegetables

My favourite greengrocers display their wares so that customers can buy in small quantities without being made to feel stingy. For entertaining choose as many different varieties as possible, in quantities to fit into your steamer baskets. For example:

INGREDIENTS

new potatoes
thin fresh asparagus in season
baby sweetcorn
cauliflower florets
carrots, cut into fingers
courgettes, cut into fingers
green beans, sliced if necessary
mange-touts *or* sugar-snap peas

Serve with a prepared herb butter, or microwave Hollandaise (see page 294) or Mustard Hollandaise (see page 295).

METHOD

1 Cook the vegetables in the steamer basket; those which will take longest to cook – as indicated in the order of the ingredients – should go in before the rest. Potatoes and thin asparagus may take 10–15 minutes to soften, mange-touts should take only 3–4 minutes.

Make sure the water under the steamer is boiling
rapidly and that the lid is tightly on the pan.
2 Drain and serve hot with a herb butter (see below) or
Hollandaise Sauce.

Herb butter

With a wooden spoon, mash together 4 oz (115 g)
softened butter, and the grated rind and juice of ½
lemon, 2 tablespoons chopped parsley* and salt and
pepper to taste. Form the herb butter into butter pats,
or a long thick roll for slicing, and leave to firm in the refrigerator.

* The parsley can be replaced by freshly chopped mint or chives,
or by a mixture of chopped fresh herbs.

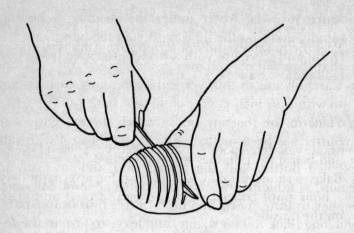

Sliced roast potatoes

A favourite recipe for those who like the crisp bits of roast potatoes.

Serves 4

Oven temperature: 200°C, 400°F, gas mark 6

Cooking time: approximately 1 hour

INGREDIENTS

4–8 medium potatoes (1–2 each, according to appetite)
2 oz (55 g) block margarine or butter
1 tablespoon oil
salt

METHOD

1 Peel the potatoes and cut a thin slice from one side so
   that they will not roll over.
2 Carefully cut in thin vertical slices along each potato
   to within ⅓ inch (1 cm) of this flat base.*
3 Place in the roasting tin in which the margarine or
   butter has been melted with the oil. Season with salt
   and brush the potatoes with the melted fat.
4 Bake, with occasional re-brushing, for approximately
   1 hour until cooked right through, brown and crisp
   on the outside.

* To do this quickly, insert a thin metal skewer horizontally ⅓ inch
(1 cm) above the base and then cut down to this skewer. Remove
before baking.

Pilaf with nuts

Serves 2

This mixture can be used as a vegetable in place of potatoes, or as a stuffing for poultry, or it can be cooked in the same pan as a roast joint so that it absorbs the juices and becomes brown and crispy. It can also be used as the stuffing mixture for peppers or courgettes (see page 38).

INGREDIENTS

½ small onion
1 tablespoon corn oil
4 tablespoons long-grain rice (or a mixture of long-grain and wild rice)
1 oz (30 g) pine nuts
1 oz (30 g) flaked or chopped almonds
11–12 fl oz (310–340 ml) hot chicken stock
½ oz (15 g) raisins, chopped
saffron (optional)

METHOD

1 Fry the chopped-up onion in the oil.
2 Add the rice and nuts and fry until light brown.
3 Stir in the stock and raisins, with a little saffron to colour, and cook with the lid on for about 20 minutes until the rice is tender and most of the liquid absorbed.

Crisp green salad

Most green salads have to be tossed in vinaigrette
dressing just before serving otherwise they soon go limp
and unappetizing. But this dressed salad stays crisp for
two or three days in a refrigerator and the acid of the
vinaigrette helps to prevent destruction of vitamin C.
You can make it even more appetizing and nourishing
by adding fresh orange slices or membrane-free orange
segments to the salad on the ensuing days.

INGREDIENTS

cucumber
salt
Chinese leaves
green pepper
chives
vinaigrette dressing (page 29)

METHOD

1 Cut the unpeeled cucumber into medium-thick slices
  and then into cubes. To crisp, scatter generously with
  salt. After 10 minutes use running cold water to wash
  away the salt through a sieve. Pat dry with kitchen
  paper.
2 Meanwhile, shred the Chinese leaves finely, chop the
  de-seeded pepper and snip the chives. Mix in the
  serving bowl, adding the cucumber.
3 Toss in vinaigrette dressing and store, covered, in the
  refrigerator.

Monty's coleslaw

The quantities given are for a buffet party, but the recipe can be halved. It keeps well for several days in the refrigerator.

INGREDIENTS

½ lb (225 g) red cabbage
½ lb (225 g) white cabbage
½ lb (225 g) carrots
½ lb (225 g) swede
2 red sweet peppers (capsicums), de-seeded
1 head celery (without leaves)
1 apple
1 firm pear
4 oz (115 g) desiccated coconut
4 oz (115 g) sultanas
4 oz (115 g) currants
4 oz (115 g) chopped mixed nuts

Salad dressing
2 fl oz (55 ml) sunflower oil
2 fl oz (55 ml) white vinegar
6 tablespoons honey
1 level tablespoon mustard powder

METHOD

1 Finely grate the red cabbage and soak, changing the water frequently until the water remains colourless.
2 Finely grate the white cabbage, carrots and swede. Chop the red peppers and celery into small pieces.

3 Finely grate the apple and pear and add the coconut, sultanas, currants and nuts, mixing well together.
4 Add all the above ingredients together and mix well.
5 Whisk the oil, vinegar and honey together and use a little of the mixture to reconstitute the mustard. Add this mustard to the oil and vinegar.
6 Pour the dressing over the salad ingredients and mix well before using or storing in a refrigerator.

Microwave hollandaise sauce

(makes over ¼ pint)

INGREDIENTS

4 oz (115 g) unsalted butter at room temperature
2 or 3 egg yolks from size 3 eggs*
2 tablespoons fresh lemon juice
salt and white pepper to taste

METHOD

1 Whisk the egg yolks in a glass jug or bowl, gradually whisking in the lemon juice.
2 Cut the softened butter into three sections. Add one third to the egg yolk mixture. Cook uncovered on High (600–700 watts) for 30 seconds.
3 Beat vigorously using a wire whisk (the butter will not be completely melted until after this beating.
4 Add the second piece of butter. Cook again for 30 seconds and repeat the procedure of beating well until the butter is absorbed into the yolks.
5 Add the third piece of butter and repeat the heating and beating procedure. Season with salt and pepper.

Note: by adding cool butter to the mixture each time, the risk of curdling is reduced, but if the sauce should curdle, add 1 tablespoon of boiling water and beat again until creamy and thick.

* This recipe was tested with either quantity and both gave satisfactory results.

Mustard hollandaise sauce

This is a quick and easy version of the classic hollandaise. Ready-made mustard saves the trouble of preparing
the usual infusion of vinegar, and melting the butter
first speeds up the thickening.

Serve warm with ham, broccoli or other steamed
vegetables.

Serves 2

INGREDIENTS

3 oz (85 g) unsalted butter
2 egg yolks (from size 3 eggs)
¼ teaspoon French mustard

You will need a small balloon whisk.

METHOD

1 Cut up the butter and melt by placing in a jug
standing in a pan of gently simmering water. When
melted put on one side.

2 In a small pan or bowl that will fit over the top of the
pan of simmering water, whisk the egg yolks with the
mustard. Continue whisking over the hot but not
boiling water until the eggs thicken.

3 Remove from the heat and gradually pour in the
warm melted butter, whisking continually to make a
sauce almost thick enough to hold its shape.

Baked salmon and spinach

Serves 2

Oven temperature: 190°C, 375°F, gas mark 5

Cooking time: 20–25 minutes

INGREDIENTS

1 lb (450 g) fresh leaf spinach *or* 10.6 oz (300 g) frozen leaf
   spinach
butter
salt, pepper and nutmeg
2 × 6 oz (170 g) pieces fillet of salmon, skinned*
lemon juice

Serve with steamed new potatoes, garnished with fresh
dill or dried dill weed.

METHOD

1 Butter 2 squares of greaseproof paper, large enough
   to parcel the salmon (butter the paper all over, and
   especially well in the centre) and place on a baking
   sheet.
2 Lift washed and trimmed fresh spinach, dripping
   wet, into a saucepan and cook gently in a tightly
   covered pan. Cook frozen spinach as directed on the
   packet.
3 Drain, chop and press as dry as possible.

* The tail end is less likely to contain bones.

4 Place a bed of spinach on each paper square. Season, dot with butter and sprinkle with salt, pepper and nutmeg.

5 Place salmon fillets on top, season and sprinkle with lemon juice, and fold the papers loosely into parcels (see illustration).

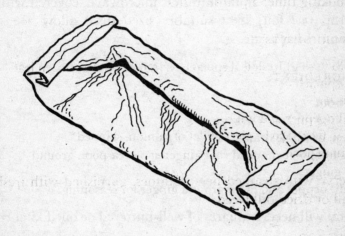

6 Bake until thoroughly cooked and succulent, not dry (approximately 20–25 minutes).

7 Unfold carefully. Serve with new potatoes, garnished with dill.

Baked trout and orange

Serves 2

Oven temperature: 190°C, 375°F, gas mark 5

Cooking time: 25 minutes. Or microwave, covered with wrap (*not* foil) in a suitably sized dish; allow 2½–3 minutes each side.

INGREDIENTS

2 trout
grated rind of ¼ orange
flesh of whole orange
½ teaspoon chopped root ginger *or* ¼ teaspoon ground ginger
salt, pepper and extra ground ginger for seasoning

You will need 2 squares of well-buttered or oiled kitchen foil.

METHOD

1 Clean the trout, wash and pat dry. Stuff the cavity with the grated orange rind, the cut-up orange flesh (reserving 2 slices for garnish) and the ginger.
2 Season and place on the foil. Fold into loose parcels.
3 Bake for 25 minutes.
4 Remove from the foil. Serve with the juices and garnish with the fresh orange slices.

Chinese fish

Serves 2

INGREDIENTS

3 tablespoons sliced spring onion (including the green part)
½ tablespoon finely chopped fresh ginger
1 small carrot, peeled
¼ small green or red pepper, seeds removed
chunk of cucumber, unpeeled
2 large or 4 small fillets of flat fish (e.g. plaice, lemon sole)
salt and pepper
1 tablespoon oil (preferably groundnut)
1 teaspoon sesame oil

Serve with rice, baby sweetcorn and mange-touts.

METHOD

1 Prepare the vegetable topping: slice the spring onions and chop the ginger; cut the carrot, pepper and cucumber into thin matchsticks.
2 Wash the fish and rub with salt and pepper. Put into a large shallow frying-pan.
3 Pour boiling water over the fish, bring back to the boil and simmer for 2 minutes.
4 Remove the pan from the heat. Cover tightly with a lid or foil and leave for 8 minutes.
5 Just before the fish is ready, heat the oils in a small frying-pan, stir in the vegetable topping and cook quickly for 1 minute. Season.
6 Drain the fish as it is lifted from the pan, and put on to warmed plates. Add the hot topping and serve.

Four-fish bake

Serves 3–4

Oven temperature: 200°C, 400°F, gas mark 6

Cooking time: approximately 25 minutes after preliminary cooking of fish

INGREDIENTS

1 lb (½ kg) potatoes, peeled
knob of butter
a few tablespoons of milk
seasoning
generous ¼ pint (140 ml) white wine
1 slice of onion
3 or 4 peppercorns
½ lb (225 g) fresh salmon fillet, skinned*
½ lb (225 g) thick fillet of haddock or halibut, skinned*
4 oz (115 g) fillet of smoked haddock
2 oz (55 g) shelled cooked prawns
chopped parsley or dill
2 teaspoons butter
2 teaspoons flour
small (5 fl oz, 140 ml) carton soured cream
1 oz (30 g) Gruyère cheese, grated
shake of cayenne pepper
parsley or dill to garnish

Serve with green beans or other green vegetable.

* The tail end is less likely to contain bones.

METHOD

1 Boil the potatoes and mash with a little butter and milk. Season to taste.

2 Meanwhile, put the wine, onion and peppercorns in a shallow pan, add all the fish, except the prawns and simmer gently. This can be done on top of the stove, in the oven or in a microwave. The fish may need to be turned once.

3 Grease an ovenproof dish which can be brought to the table. Lift large flakes or chunks of the lightly cooked fish into the bottom of the casserole, carefully removing any bones.

4 Stir in the prawns, plus the chopped-up, cooked onion. Add chopped parsley or dill for extra flavour.

5 Discard the peppercorns from the wine in the pan. With a spoon, make a paste by rubbing the butter into the flour (*beurre manié*). Drop small quantities into the hot wine, stirring in just enough over low heat to thicken into a sauce; a little more wine can be added if too much has evaporated in the cooking.

6 Remove from the heat, stir in the soured cream and reheat gently without boiling. Stir this warm creamy sauce into the fish.

7 Cover with the creamed potatoes. There should be about twice as much fish as there is potato.

8 Sprinkle with the cheese and a little cayenne pepper. Dot with butter and bake for about 25 minutes until it is well heated through and the cheese is golden. Garnish with parsley or dill.

Chicken breast stuffed with mango or kiwi fruit

Serves 4

Oven temperature: 180°C, 350°F, gas mark 4

Cooking time: 30–40 minutes

INGREDIENTS

1 ripe mango (or two kiwi fruit)
4 skinless, boned chicken breasts
salt and pepper
knob of butter
chopped parsley or basil
½ pint (285 ml) milk
1 oz (30 g) butter or margarine
1 oz (30 g) flour
medium-dry sherry

Serve with steamed vegetables.

METHOD

1 Peel and slice the mango or kiwi fruit and use a few slices to stuff the chicken breasts. Season lightly and place in a well-greased casserole dish.
2 Dot with butter, sprinkle generously with chopped parsley or basil and place the rest of the fruit around the chicken pieces.
3 Bake, with the lid on the casserole, for 30–40 minutes, according to the thickness of the chicken.

4 Dish the chicken on to serving plates and keep warm.
5 Make a white sauce from the milk, butter and flour.
6 Mash into it the remaining fruit and juices from the dish, flavour with a dash of sherry; season.
7 Pour over the stuffed chicken and serve immediately.

Honey mustard chicken

Serves 6 (or freeze some portions for use within 1 month)

Oven temperature: 200°C, 400°F, gas mark 6

Cooking time: ½ an hour or longer

INGREDIENTS

6 boned chicken breasts
2 dessertspoons softened butter
2 generous tablespoons whole-grain mustard
2 tablespoons clear honey

METHOD

1 Mix the butter, mustard and honey together and pour over the chicken in the casserole.
2 Bake for at least 30 minutes. This is an easy-going recipe and it will not be overcooked if it is left for about ¾ hour. Serve, or cool and freeze.

Reheat from frozen at 200°C, 400°F, gas mark 6 for 50–60 minutes.

Lemon and orange chicken

Can be served hot but it is just as good cold.

Serves 2

Oven temperature: 180°C, 350°F, gas mark 4

Cooking time: 35–40 minutes in the oven, after a preliminary 10 minutes frying

INGREDIENTS

2 chicken joints
3 tablespoons lemon juice
3 tablespoons orange juice
3 tablespoons fine matzo meal, or plain flour
¼ teaspoon salt
¼ teaspoon paprika
5–6 grinds black pepper
2 tablespoons corn oil
½ tablespoon grated lemon (or mixed orange and lemon) rind
2 tablespoons demerara sugar
4 tablespoons chicken stock
2 thin slices lemon
2 thin slices orange

METHOD

1 Marinade the chicken for several hours, or overnight, in the lemon and orange juice, turning occasionally.
2 Drain and pat dry with kitchen paper.

3 Place the meal or flour and the seasonings in a bag and shake the chicken joints so that they are well covered.

4 Fry in the oil until browned and crisp on both sides; this may take about 10 minutes.

5 Transfer to a shallow baking pan, sprinkle with the grated rind and sugar. Pour the stock around and place a thin slice of lemon and orange on top of each joint.

6 Bake, with the lid on, for 35–40 minutes until thoroughly cooked.

If you are looking for a celebratory dinner for two for Christmas (or any other special occasion), I suggest one of the following three recipes, served with the usual trimmings such as Brussels Sprouts and Chestnuts (page 73), apple sauce or Cranberry and Marmalade Sauce (page 25), and Sliced Roast Potatoes (page 288).

Sherried turkey with lemons

Serves 2 (for 3–4 portions increase the amount of turkey and onion but keep to the same amount for the rest of the ingredients)

INGREDIENTS

1 oz (30 g) butter
1 tablespoon oil
2 turkey steaks or escalopes
4 oz (115 g) onion, sliced
1 tablespoon flour
½ pint (285 ml) chicken stock
3 tablespoons medium-dry sherry
juice and finely grated rind of ½ lemon
salt and freshly ground pepper
½ lemon, sliced
fresh chives, finely snipped

Serve with bread rolls (to help mop up the delicious gravy).

METHOD

1 Heat the butter and oil and brown the turkey. Remove and keep hot.
2 In the same pan, fry the onion gently until soft.
3 Stir in the flour and cook for 2 minutes, and then gradually add the stock.
4 Bring to the boil, stirring continuously, then add the sherry, turkey, finely grated rind, lemon juice and seasoning.
5 Cover and simmer gently for 25–30 minutes.
6 Garnish with lemon slices and chives.

Poussin with Stilton and port

Serves 2

Oven temperature: 200°C, 400°F, gas mark 6

Cooking time: approximately 1 hour

INGREDIENTS

2 oz (55 g) blue Stilton
1½ oz (45 g) low or medium-fat soft cheese
2 poussins
1 oz (30 g) butter
salt and freshly ground black pepper
3 oz (85 g) button mushrooms, trimmed and halved unless
    tiny
4 fl oz (115 ml) chicken stock
5 tablespoons ruby port
1 tablespoon redcurrant jelly
1 teaspoon cornflour

METHOD

1 In a bowl, mash together the Stilton and the soft
   cheese.
2 Carefully separate the skin from the breast meat of
   the poussins (I find this is best done by using the blunt
   handle of a teaspoon).
3 Push the cheese mixture between the flesh and the
   skin, spreading it as evenly as possible. Secure the
   small flap of skin with a wooden cocktail stick.

4 Place the poussins in an ovenproof dish, melt half of the butter and brush it over the birds. Season and cook for 40 minutes, basting twice during cooking.

5 Meanwhile, heat the rest of the butter in a saucepan, add the mushrooms and cook for 3–4 minutes. Pour in the chicken stock and simmer until the mushrooms are tender. Remove with a slotted spoon and set aside.

6 After the preliminary 40 minutes, pour the port over the poussins and continue to cook for a further 10–15 minutes until golden and cooked right through.

7 Remove the poussins on to the serving platter and keep hot while finishing the sauce:
(a) Strain the port juices from the fat in the pan.
(b) Stir the redcurrant jelly into the chicken stock in the saucepan, add the port juices and the mushrooms and simmer 2–3 minutes.
(c) Blend the cornflour with a tablespoon of water, and use to thicken the sauce.

8 Pour this mushroom sauce over the poussins.

Roast duckling with citrus gravy

Serves 2

Oven temperature: 200°C, 400°F, gas mark 6

Cooking time: 60–75 minutes

INGREDIENTS

2 duckling breast quarters
salt
2 tablespoons granulated sugar
1 teaspoon balsamic vinegar
4 tablespoons juice from pink grapefruit
4 tablespoons fresh orange juice
1 teaspoon cornflour

Serve with roast potatoes, favourite vegetables and apple sauce (stewed apple mashed with nutmeg, and a little sugar if very tart).

METHOD

1 Prick the duckling all over with a fork and rub the skin with a little salt.
2 Place on a trivet and roast for 60–75 minutes until cooked right through and crisp and brown on the outside.
3 Take 2 tablespoons of the duckling fat from the pan and heat gently in a frying-pan with the sugar.

4 After a few moments add the vinegar and fruit juices. Thicken with the cornflour, mixed to a thin cream with a little water. Serve this tangy citrus sauce as a gravy poured over the roast duckling.

With apple and onion sauce

Peel core and slice thinly one or two large cooking apples. Put into a small saucepan with half a peeled, thinly sliced onion and two or three tablespoons of sherry. Cover and simmer very gently, stirring occasionally, until it softens to a pulp. Add a knob of butter and sweeten to taste with brown sugar. Serve separately in a warmed sauceboat.

Beef and raisin meatballs in lemon sauce

Serves 3–4 (makes 12 meatballs)

INGREDIENTS

1 egg (size 3)
1 lb (450 g) minced beef
1 small onion, finely chopped
2 tablespoons raisins
2 tablespoons walnuts, chopped
1 pinch of ground allspice
salt and pepper
4 sprigs parsley, finely chopped
½ pint (285 ml) beef stock
2 teaspoons lemon juice
For sauce
2 teaspoons cornflour
5 fl oz (140 ml) natural yogurt
extra chopped parsley

Serve with rice or noodles and a green vegetable.

METHOD

1 Beat the egg in a large mixing bowl.
2 Add the minced beef, onion, raisins, walnuts, allspice, salt, pepper and parsley. Mix well. Shape into meatballs with floured hands.

3 Pour the well-seasoned stock and lemon juice into a heavy-based saucepan and bring to the boil. Add the meatballs, cover, and then simmer gently, turning once, for about 45 minutes, until the meat is tender.

4 Remove from the liquid and place in a warmed serving dish. Pour off the fat from the surface of the stock in the pan.

5 *To make the sauce*, mix the cornflour to a smooth cream with a little water. Add to the stock, stir and simmer until thickened. Stir in the yogurt and parsley, reheat gently without boiling and pour over the meatballs. Serve immediately.

Creamed pork

Serves 4

INGREDIENTS

1 tablespoon oil
½ oz (15 g) butter
12 oz (340 g) lean pork (cubed)
1 onion, chopped
1 level teaspoon paprika
1 level tablespoon flour
½ pint (285 ml) chicken stock
5 tablespoons sherry
1 teaspoon tomato purée
salt and pepper
4 oz (115 g) mushrooms, sliced
1 level tablespoon cornflour
3 tablespoons double cream

Serve with fresh broad beans or other green vegetable.

METHOD

1 Fry pork in fats to brown lightly. Remove and drain.
2 Fry onion and paprika for 2 minutes, add flour and cook for a further minute.
3 Remove from heat, add stock, sherry and tomato purée. Simmer until thickened.
4 Season, add pork and mushrooms, simmer for 40 minutes. Before serving, blend cornflour to a thin paste with a little cold water; add to pan.
5 Re-boil, stir in the cream, but do not allow to boil again. Serve immediately.

Fillet steak with cream and brandy

A luxury dish prepared in a few minutes.

Serves 2

INGREDIENTS

2 large or 4 small fillet steaks, cut ½ inch (1 cm) thick
flour seasoned with salt and black pepper
knob of butter
dash of brandy
3–4 fl oz (85–115 ml) white wine
1 ½ teaspoons whole-grain mustard
3–4 sun-dried tomatoes, cut small*
5 fl oz (140 ml) double cream
salt and pepper

Serve with steamed new potatoes, green beans and baby sweetcorn or other preferred vegetable.

METHOD

1 Coat the steaks in seasoned flour and fry for 2–3 minutes on each side in a lightly buttered pan (adjust the timing according to rareness required).
2 Pour on the brandy and wine and stir in the mustard and tomatoes.
3 While it is still bubbling hot, pour on the cream, heat very gently without boiling and taste for seasoning.

* These can be bought in jars, preserved in oil. They have a deeper colour and a stronger flavour than fresh tomatoes.

Sweet and savoury minced beef

This recipe was given to me by a friend who first cooked it at a 'retirement' cookery class. It is a delicious mixture of sweet and savoury: good family fare, but also suitable for a dinner party.

4–6 servings

INGREDIENTS

2 large onions, chopped
2 tablespoons oil
2 lb (900 g) minced beef
14 oz (400 g) can peeled tomatoes
1 large red pepper, de-seeded and chopped
1 medium green pepper, de-seeded and chopped
2 medium cooking apples, peeled, cored and chopped
2 oz (55 g) raisins
12 stuffed olives, halved
¼ teaspoon cinnamon
salt and pepper
large pinch chilli powder
1 small can tomato purée, or to taste

Topping
2 oz (55 g) flaked almonds, lightly browned (without fat) in a frying-pan or under the grill

METHOD

1 Sauté the onions in the oil. Add the mince and continue to fry until no pink shows.

2 Add the chopped-up tomatoes with some of the juice (add more juice if necessary as it cooks). Stir in the peppers, apples, raisins, olives, cinnamon, seasonings and tomato purée.

3 Simmer for 1 hour (in the oven or on top of the stove).

4 Sprinkle the browned almonds on top just before serving.

Herb-roasted lamb

Serves 2

Oven temperature: 180°C, 350°F, gas mark 4–5

Cooking time: approximately 50 minutes

INGREDIENTS

¾–1 lb (340–450 g) rack of lamb (a joint of 4–6 best end
  neck chops)
salt and pepper
½–1 tablespoon redcurrant jelly
½ teaspoon dried rosemary (or 2 fresh sprigs)
½ teaspoon dried oregano (or 2 fresh sprigs)

Serve with extra redcurrant jelly, new potatoes and a
fresh green vegetable.

METHOD

1 Place the seasoned joint on a rack in a roasting tin
  and roast for 30 minutes.
2 Remove from the oven, spread with the jelly and
  sprinkle with the herbs.
3 Return to the oven for a further 20 minutes, or until
  cooked to your liking.

Note: to serve more people, cook leg or shoulder of
lamb, or a boneless rolled joint. For medium-cooked
meat allow 25 minutes per pound, plus 25 mins. For
well-done meat, allow 30 minutes per pound, plus 30
mins. Spread with the jelly and herbs for the last 20
minutes.

Almond pudding

Serves 8–10

Oven temperature: 180°C, 350°F, gas mark 4

Cooking time: 45 minutes to 1 hour

You will need a 2 pint (1.1 litre) soufflé dish or oval pudding dish.

INGREDIENTS

6 eggs (3 eggs size 2, plus 3 eggs size 3)
8 oz (225 g) caster sugar
8 oz (225 g) ground almonds

Serve with dried fruit compote or fresh fruit salad.

METHOD

1 Whisk the yolks with the sugar until thick and creamy.
2 Whisk the whites to fairly stiff peaks.
3 Very carefully fold the sieved ground almonds into the egg yolk and sugar mixture, keeping it moist with a tablespoon or two of the beaten egg whites.
4 Fold in the rest of the egg whites.
5 Turn into the well-greased dish and bake. It should be just firm to the touch when tested, like a sponge cake.

This almond sponge will sink a little in the middle as it cools but this is a sign of lightness, not heaviness. Dust lightly with caster sugar when cold.

Banana pudding

This is a family favourite sent to me from a good-cook friend in Australia. It contains no eggs, butter or sugar. To turn it into an easily made alternative to a Christmas pudding she recommends adding 1 egg and replacing 2–3 tablespoons of the milk with 2–3 tablespoons of brandy.

You will need a 1½ pint (0.9 litre) pudding basin.

INGREDIENTS

1 teaspoon bicarbonate of soda
1 teacup milk
2 teacups dried, mixed fruit, including some cooking dates
2½ teacups soft breadcrumbs
1 large (or 2 small) very ripe banana, mashed
a few drops lemon juice

METHOD

1 Dissolve the bicarbonate of soda in a little of the milk, then mix all the ingredients well together.
2 Steam in a greased covered pudding basin for 2½–3 hours.

Note: this pudding freezes well for several months and can then be defrosted and re-boiled for about an hour.

Brandy butter (spiced)

The better the brandy, the better the taste!

Because of the spices, this is well flavoured, needing less sugar than the usual recipes.

INGREDIENTS

8 oz (225 g) unsalted butter
12 oz (340 g) caster sugar
½ level teaspoon ground nutmeg
½ level teaspoon cinnamon
6 tablespoons (plus!) brandy – or rum if you prefer rum
  butter

METHOD

1 *Thoroughly* cream the butter, sugar and spices together (easiest in bowl of electric mixer).
2 With the motor still running, *gradually* incorporate the brandy, of course tasting very frequently until it reaches the desired strength. But be warned: if you overdo it (adding, not tasting) the excess liquor may seep out.

Brûlée creams (uncooked)

Serves 6

INGREDIENTS

fresh fruit, e.g. strawberries, raspberries, kiwi fruit,
   bananas*
caster sugar
Cointreau or rum according to fruit used (optional)
5 fl oz (140 ml) whipping cream
5 fl oz (140 ml) low-fat natural yogurt
golden granulated sugar, or demerara sugar

METHOD

1 Prepare the fruit (wash and slice if necessary) and
   sprinkle with caster sugar; leave until the juices run
   and then drain.
2 Sprinkle with Cointreau or rum if used and leave for
   a short while for the flavour to penetrate.
3 Whip the cream until stiff, then add the yogurt and
   whip again.
4 Place fruit in individual ramekins or a soufflé dish
   and spoon the cream mixture over the top.
5 Sprinkle thickly with the golden or brown sugar and
   refrigerate, preferably overnight.

* This is also a delicious way of using the fruit in liqueur often sold
at Christmas.

Cherry frangipane flan

Serves 8

Oven temperature: 190°C, 375°F, gas mark 5

Cooking time: about 45 minutes

INGREDIENTS

1 shortcrust or sweet pastry 10 inch (25 cm) flan case*
raspberry jam
2 × 14½ oz (415 g) cans stoneless red cherries
3 oz (85 g) ground almonds
3 oz (85 g) soft margarine
3 oz (85 g) granulated or caster sugar
1 tablespoon flour
2 eggs, size 3
icing sugar

METHOD

1 Spread the uncooked pastry case with jam.
2 Cover with a layer of drained cherries.
3 Beat the almonds, margarine, sugar, flour and eggs.
4 Spread over the filled flan and bake. Towards the end, it may be necessary to cover with greaseproof paper to protect the top from over-browning.
5 Serve warm, or reheated, sprinkled with sieved icing sugar.

* This can be made ahead and frozen raw (see pages 326–7). It only takes an hour or so to defrost before filling and baking.

Cherries jubilee

Serves 3–4

INGREDIENTS

15 oz (425 g) can stoneless black cherries*
a dash of cherry brandy or kirsch (optional)
¾ teaspoon cornflour
scoops of vanilla ice-cream

METHOD

1 Just before you sit down to the meal, put the cherries with their juice (and the liqueur if used) in a saucepan. Leave, covered, to heat very gently.
2 Mix the cornflour to a thin cream with cold water in a small bowl.
3 When ready to serve the dessert, stir the cornflour and add a little of the hot juice. Return to the pan with the cherries and simmer until thickened.
4 Place scoops of vanilla ice-cream into individual serving bowls and pour the hot cherries and thickened juice over the top. Serve immediately.

* Cherries with stones may be used, as long as your guests are warned!

Peaches, stuffed and baked

Serves 4

Oven temperature: 180°C, 350°F, gas mark 4

Cooking time: approximately 20 minutes

INGREDIENTS

4 free-stone fresh peaches
8 *amaretti* biscuit halves, crushed*
2 teaspoons chopped nuts
4–6 glacé cherries, chopped
knob of butter
a little fresh lemon juice
a pinch of nutmeg
a few spoonfuls of medium-sweet sherry for basting

Serve with single cream or yogurt.

METHOD

1 Halve and peel the peaches, and remove the stones.
2 Fill the cavity with a mixture of *amaretti* crumbs, nuts and cherries.
3 Flake a little butter on top and sprinkle with lemon juice and nutmeg.
4 Bake for 20 minutes, basting twice with a little sherry.
5 Serve warm.

* Macaroons or ratafia biscuits can be used instead, but I prefer the stronger flavour of the *amaretti*.

Gilly's sweet pastry

This makes sufficient for two 10 inch flan cases or three 8 inch flan cases; or portions of the pastry can be used for small tartlet cases

INGREDIENTS

1 lb (450 g) plain flour
10 oz (285 g) unsalted butter (firm but not fridge-cold), roughly chopped
4 oz (115 g) caster sugar
yolks of 2 large eggs (size 2)

METHOD

1 For speed, place all ingredients in the bowl of an electric food mixer and beat until it just begins to form a ball. **If using a food processor**, first process the flour, butter and sugar to resemble coarse breadcrumbs, then add the egg yolks to form a ball around the knife. Do not over-mix.

2 Gather together, and divide into usable sizes. Wrap in foil and refrigerate briefly before use *or* freeze uncooked pastry made up in flan cases.

Tips
To roll out easily, remove from the refrigerator and return to room temperature. Roll out between two sheets of clingfilm.

Remove the top sheet of clingfilm and invert the flan tin lightly on the pastry; tip the pastry over into the flan tin, remove the second sheet of clingfilm, and press and cut the pastry into shape.

Alternatively, for easy handling: make a cross with a knife in the rolled-out pastry round, cutting it into four sections. Lift each section separately into the flan dish (using a fish slice) and reassemble into the round by pressing the edges firmly together. Trim. Place back in the refrigerator to become firm again before filling.

Before filling raw pastry cases with fruit, sprinkle lightly with ground almonds or semolina; this will help to absorb the juices of the fruit as it cooks, and keeps the pastry crisp.

Frozen raw flan cases are ready to be filled an hour or so after removal from the freezer.

Melon and grape dessert

Other fruits can be used, such as cut-up pineapple and stem ginger, adding some stem ginger syrup to the lemon juice to flavour the sugar syrup. For this combination, I frost the glasses with orange colouring (or a mixture of yellow and red).

INGREDIENTS

1 honeydew melon
1 bunch seedless green grapes
½ cup granulated or caster sugar
juice of ½–1 lemon
extra caster sugar
a few drops of green or yellow food colouring

METHOD

1 Cut the melon in half and discard the seeds. Spoon out into a bowl with a melon baller.
2 Wash the grapes and add to the melon balls.
3 Heat 1 cup water and the sugar in a small saucepan, stirring until dissolved. Boil rapidly for 5 minutes. Add the lemon juice.
4 Shake some extra caster sugar on to kitchen paper and colour with a few drops of food colouring well rubbed in with the back of a teaspoon.
5 Dip the rims of serving glasses briefly into the warm lemon syrup, then rub into the caster sugar to frost the rims of the glasses. Store in a cool place until needed.

6 While the syrup is still warm pour it over the fruit.
Cool and refrigerate.

7 Just before the meal, spoon the fruit and syrup into
the glasses, carefully avoiding the frosted rims.

Pears in blackberry sauce

Serves 4

INGREDIENTS

4 pears
8 oz (225 g) blackberries
3 tablespoons honey
sugar (optional)
cassis (optional)

METHOD

1 Peel, core and quarter the pears.

2 Warm the blackberries and honey together in a saucepan, and poach the pears very gently in this mixture,
turning occasionally, until tender.

3 Remove the pears into a deep serving dish.

4 Sieve the blackberries, return the purée to the pan
and boil, sweetening if necessary, until it becomes a
thicker syrup. At this stage it can be flavoured with
cassis (blackcurrant liqueur).

5 Pour over the pears and serve hot or cold.

Raspberry dessert (chilled)

Serves 4 – quantities can be doubled to serve 8

Oven temperature: 170°C, 325°F, gas mark 3

Cooking time: 25 minutes

You will need 4 × 3 inch (7.5 cm) ramekins, or an 8 inch (20 cm) loose-bottomed or spring-form tin if making double quantities.

The flavour of this dessert improves if it is made the day before serving.

INGREDIENTS

8 oz (225 g) fresh, frozen or canned raspberries
2 oz (55 g) digestive biscuits
scant 1 oz (20 g) unsalted butter or margarine
2 × 5 fl oz (140 ml) cartons sour cream
1 1/2–2 oz (45–55 g) caster sugar

METHOD

1 Defrost or drain the raspberries if using frozen or canned.
2 Crush the biscuits, mix with the butter or margarine and press into the base of the ramekins or the tin.
3 Mix the sour cream, sugar and raspberries lightly together. Spoon on to the biscuit crust and bake for 25 minutes.
4 When cooled, leave in the refrigerator before serving.

Cheese and fruit kebabs

Although dessert fruits and a cheese board are generally welcome at the end of a meal, small amounts look stingy and a generous choice often results in waste. This is an alternative.

Choose small blocks of two or three types of cheese (e.g. Cheddar, Emmental, Stilton) and a small amount of fruits. Choose from, for example, seedless grapes, melon, pineapple, pear and apple (dipped in lemon juice), plums, peaches, nectarines, strawberries. Thread a mixture of cheese and fruit on long kebab sticks, allowing two or three kebabs per guest. Pick up the kebabs with the fingers and nibble daintily . . .

Or serve **Small Fruit Kebabs** on cocktail sticks: melon ball, strawberry and green grape look attractive.

Mini-fruits platter

For after-dinner fruit nibbles, arrange bite-sized portions of fruit on a large platter. Either wash them just before serving, or provide small dipping bowls of water, with a thin slice of lemon floating on top.

Choose fruits according to the season, for example: seedless grapes, cut in tiny bunches of two or three; segments of seedless clementines, satsumas or oranges; peeled slices or wedges of kiwi fruit; cherries on stalk; strawberries on stalk; peeled and stoned lychees; cape gooseberries; small sweet plums; sweet dessert gooseberries.

Decorate the platter with dried fruits and nuts such as dried figs, apricots or prunes, including the sweet, sticky varieties and some fresh dates if available, and assorted nuts including pistachio, monkey nuts, pecans, walnuts, brazil nuts and almonds (either crack from their shells or provide nutcrackers and plates for the empty shells).

Plated fruit salad

A simple but decorative dessert to be served instead of a heavier pudding.

INGREDIENTS

1 cup water
½ cup sugar
½ lemon or small orange (grated rind and juice) *or* liqueur
  (Cointreau, Grand Marnier or cherry brandy)
choice of decorative fruits, e.g. small sweet melon, mango,
  kiwi fruit, strawberries, cherries, seedless grapes

METHOD

1 Make a thick syrup by bringing the water and sugar to the boil, stirring, then continuing to boil without stirring for 5 minutes. Stir in the lemon or orange rind and juice, or liqueur to taste. Chill.
2 Prepare the fruit and cut long slices to make a fan of the larger fruit on individual dessert plates. Intersperse with the kiwi and other smaller fruits.
3 Spoon the syrup over the fruit fans and refrigerate until served.

Bacchanalian dried-fruit salad

INGREDIENTS

½ lb (225 g) dried apricots
¼ lb (115 g) dried dates, stoned
¼ lb (115 g) prunes, stoned
¼ lb (115 g) sultanas
1 oz (30 g) currants
1 apple (preferably Granny Smith), diced small
1 oz (30 g) coarse desiccated coconut
extra desiccated coconut for top layer
sweet sherry

You will need a wide-mouthed jar with a close-fitting lid.

METHOD

1 Mix all the fruits together and place in the jar.
2 Fill with the sweet sherry until all the fruit is covered.
3 Place an additional thin layer of desiccated coconut over the fruit to reduce sherry/air contact.
4 Leave until the apricots and sultanas have swelled with the sherry. This could take a few weeks, but after that the mixture can be kept for several months.

Preserved orange slices

This is a tangy preserve to accompany poultry, game or fish.

INGREDIENTS

4 seedless oranges
1 lb (450 g) sugar
4 fl oz (115 ml) wine vinegar
1 stick cinnamon
5 cloves

You will need a wide-mouthed glass preserving jar. I use a jar with a glass stopper for an airtight seal.

METHOD

1 Peel the oranges and slice them rather more than ¼ inch (6 mm) thick – if too thin they may break up.
2 Put in a pan with just sufficient water to cover the slices and the peel when gently pressed down. Simmer for 50–60 minutes.
3 With a slotted spoon, remove the orange slices, discarding the peel.
4 To the water, add the sugar, vinegar, spices and 2 fl oz (55 ml) water. Boil for 5 minutes.
5 Replace the orange slices in the pan and simmer until the fruit becomes transparent (but do not let the syrup become too hot).
6 Pack the slices into the jar, pour the syrup over, seal and store.

Pickled prunes

These are particularly good to serve with pork, goose, duck or cold turkey. Or they can be used instead of black olives for a garnish.

INGREDIENTS

8 oz (225 g) pitted prunes
½ pint (285 ml) white or brown vinegar
8 oz (225 g) demerara sugar
20 cloves *or* 3 inch (7.5 cm) cinnamon stick

METHOD

1 Put all the ingredients into a bowl, adding ¼ pint (140 ml) water, stir and leave to soak overnight.
2 Transfer to a saucepan and cook gently until tender, with the lid on.
3 Cool and lift away from the liquid and spices. Store in a screw-top jar.

Index

Discover more about our forthcoming books through Penguin's FREE newspaper...

Penguin
Quarterly

It's packed with:

- exciting features
- author interviews
- previews & reviews
- books from your favourite films & TV series
- exclusive competitions & much, much more...

READ MORE IN PENGUIN

In every corner of the world, on every subject under the sun, Penguin represents quality and variety – the very best in publishing today.

For complete information about books available from Penguin – including Puffins, Penguin Classics and Arkana – and how to order them, write to us at the appropriate address below. Please note that for copyright reasons the selection of books varies from country to country.

In the United Kingdom: Please write to *Dept. JC, Penguin Books Ltd, FREEPOST, West Drayton, Middlesex UB7 0BR*

If you have any difficulty in obtaining a title, please send your order with the correct money, plus ten per cent for postage and packaging, to *PO Box No. 11, West Drayton, Middlesex UB7 0BR*

In the United States: Please write to *Penguin USA Inc., 375 Hudson Street, New York, NY 10014*

In Canada: Please write to *Penguin Books Canada Ltd, 10 Alcorn Avenue, Suite 300, Toronto, Ontario M4V 3B2*

In Australia: Please write to *Penguin Books Australia Ltd, 487 Maroondah Highway, Ringwood, Victoria 3134*

In New Zealand: Please write to *Penguin Books (NZ) Ltd,182–190 Wairau Road, Private Bag, Takapuna, Auckland 9*

In India: Please write to *Penguin Books India Pvt Ltd, 706 Eros Apartments, 56 Nehru Place, New Delhi 110 019*

In the Netherlands: Please write to *Penguin Books Netherlands B.V., Keizersgracht 231 NL–1016 DV Amsterdam*

In Germany: Please write to *Penguin Books Deutschland GmbH, Friedrichstrasse 10–12, W–6000 Frankfurt/Main 1*

In Spain: Please write to *Penguin Books S. A., C. San Bernardo 117–6° E–28015 Madrid*

In Italy: Please write to *Penguin Italia s.r.l., Via Felice Casati 20, I–20124 Milano*

In France: Please write to *Penguin France S. A., 17 rue Lejeune, F–31000 Toulouse*

In Japan: Please write to *Penguin Books Japan, Ishikiribashi Building, 2–5–4, Suido, Tokyo 112*

In Greece: Please write to *Penguin Hellas Ltd, Dimocritou 3, GR–106 71 Athens*

In South Africa: Please write to *Longman Penguin Southern Africa (Pty) Ltd, Private Bag X08, Bertsham 2013*

READ MORE IN PENGUIN

A SELECTION OF FOOD AND COOKERY BOOKS

The Fratelli Camisa Cookery Book   Elizabeth Camisa

From antipasti to zabaglione, from the origins of gorgonzola to the storage of salami, an indispensable guide to real Italian home cooking from Elizabeth Camisa of the famous Fratelli Camisa delicatessen in Soho's Berwick Street.

A Table in Tuscany   Leslie Forbes

With authentic recipes and beautiful illustrations, artist and cook Leslie Forbes evokes the rich flavour of Tuscany, from its Renaissance palaces to its robust red Chianti. More than a cookery book and more than mere travel writing, *A Table in Tuscany* is a culinary odyssey.

The Food and Cooking of Eastern Europe   Lesley Chamberlain

Diverse, appetising and often surprisingly sophisticated, the cuisine of Eastern Europe goes far beyond the goulash and beetroot soup familiar to the West. From the refreshing fruit soups of Hungary to the fish dishes of Dalmatia, this is a fascinating tour of Eastern gastronomy.

Chinese Food   Kenneth Lo

'From a Chinese breakfast (*congee* rice, pickled eggs, meat wool, jellied and pickled meats, roasted peanuts and "oil stick" doughnuts) to a feast poetically called Autumn on the Lower Yangtze, Mr Lo takes us brilliantly through a cuisine which it is not frivolous to call a civilization' – *Sunday Times*

Indian Cookery   Dharamjit Singh

Indian cookery is a rich and diverse cuisine steeped in tradition that goes back centuries. Many of the dishes comprise subtle combinations of spices or delicate use of herbs to give them their unique flavours, and recipes have often been handed down from one generation to the next.

More Easy Cooking for One or Two   Louise Davies

This charming book, full of ideas and easy recipes, offers even the novice cook good wholesome food with the minimum of effort.

READ MORE IN PENGUIN

A SELECTION OF FOOD AND COOKERY BOOKS

Traditional Jamaican Cookery   Norma Benghiat

Reflecting Arawak, Spanish, African, Jewish, English, French, East Indian and Chinese influences, the exciting recipes in this definitive book range from the lavish eating of the old plantocracy to imaginative and ingenious slave and peasant dishes.

Cooking in a Bedsitter   Katharine Whitehorn
Completely Revised Edition

Practical, light-hearted and full of bright ideas, *Cooking in a Bedsitter* will lure you away from the frying pan and tin-opener towards a healthier, more varied range of delicious dishes.

Simple Vegetarian Meals   Rosamond Richardson

Vegetarian food offers an exciting range of flavours and textures. It can be light and summery or rich and warming, homely or exotic. In this inspired book Rosamond Richardson explores all these aspects of vegetarian cooking, emphasizing the simplest, freshest dishes that are imaginative, economical and easy to prepare for one or two people.

Jane Grigson's Fruit Book   Jane Grigson

An alphabetical guide to fruit, from apple, apricot and arbutus to sorb apple, strawberry and water-melon. 'I take as much pleasure in reading Jane Grigson's lyrical yet well-researched and intriguing introductions to each subject as I do in executing her recipes, or merely eating the fruit she writes so well about' – *Observer*

Malaysian Cookery   Rafi Fernandez

A step-by-step guide to the intoxicating, fragrant, colourful cuisine of Malaysia: the origins of its three distinct culinary strands, traditional cooking techniques and customs, where to buy the more exotic ingredients – and a mouthwatering selection of recipes.

READ MORE IN PENGUIN

A SELECTION OF FOOD AND COOKERY BOOKS

The New Vegetarian Epicure Anna Thomas

The Vegetarian Epicure, now a classic cookery book, confirmed beyond question that non-meat meals can be luxurious, delicious and exciting. This new volume offers more culinary adventures, drawn this time from Anna Thomas's travels.

The Book of Latin American Cooking Elisabeth Lambert Ortiz

Elisabeth Lambert Ortiz introduces the reader to the subtle marriages of texture and flavour that distinguish this colourful cuisine. Try Mayan chicken, beef in fruit sauce, savoury green banana cake or coconut custard – the results can be as successful as they are unexpected.

Simple French Food Richard Olney

'There is no other book about food that is anything like it ... essential and exciting reading for cooks, of course, but it is also a book for eaters ... its pages brim over with invention' – Paul Levy in the *Observer*

English Bread and Yeast Cookery Elizabeth David

'Here is a real book, written with authority and enthusiasm – a collection of history, investigation, comment, recipes' – Jane Grigson

The Chocolate Book Helge Rubinstein

'Fact-filled celebration of the cocoa bean with toothsome recipes from turkey in chilli and chocolate sauce to brownies and chocolate grog' – *Mail on Sunday*. 'Crammed with mouth-watering puddings, drinks, cakes and confectionery' – *Guardian*

The Cookery of England Elisabeth Ayrton

Her fascinating and beautifully compiled history and recipe book of English cooking from the fifteenth century to the present day is ' a lovely book, which could restore pride in our English kitchens' – *The Times Literary Supplement*

READ MORE IN PENGUIN

FROM THE COOKERY LIBRARY

The Dinner Party Book Patricia Lousada

The Dinner Party Book hands you the magic key to entertaining without days of panic or last minute butterflies. The magic lies in cooking each course ahead, so that you can enjoy yourself along with your guests.

French Provincial Cooking Elizabeth David

'It is difficult to think of any home that can do without Elizabeth David's *French Provincial Cooking* … One could cook for a lifetime on the book alone' – *Observer*. 'Elizabeth David must have done more than anyone for British home cooking in the past twenty-five years'– *Sunday Times*

A New Book of Middle Eastern Food Claudia Roden

'This is one of those rare cookery books that is a work of cultural anthropology and Mrs Roden's standards of scholarship are so high as to ensure that it has permanent value' – Paul Levy in the *Observer*

Charcuterie and French Pork Cookery Jane Grigson

'Fully comprehensive … a detailed and enlightening insight into the preparation and cooking of pork. Altogether a unique book' – *Wine and Food*. 'The research is detailed, the recounting lively, the information fascinating' – *The Times*

The French Family Feast Mireille Johnston

Recreate the mouth-watering stews, delicious aromas and warm ambience of a convivial get-together in a traditional french home. 'Mireille Johnston has that rare combination of qualities, exceptional enthusiasm, remarkable taste, a sound knowledge of and the ability to translate kitchen techniques … a marvellous compendium of fine, easy to understand recipes' – Craig Claiborne

READ MORE IN PENGUIN

FROM THE COOKERY LIBRARY

North Atlantic Seafood   Alan Davidson

'A classic work of reference and a cook's delight' (*The Times Educational Supplement*) from the world's greatest expert on fish cookery. 'Mr Davidson has a gift for conveying memorable information in a way so effortless that his book makes lively reading for its own sake' – Elizabeth David

The Foods and Wines of Spain   Penelope Casas

'I have not come across a book before that captures so well the unlikely medieval mix of Eastern and Northern, earthy and fine, rare and deeply familiar ingredients that make up the Spanish kitchen' – *Harpers and Queen*. 'The definitive book on Spanish cooking … a jewel in the crown of culinary literature' – Craig Claiborne

An Omelette and a Glass of Wine   Elizabeth David

'She has the intelligence, subtlety, sensuality, courage and creative force of the true artist' – *Wine and Food*. 'Her pieces are so entertaining, so original, often witty, critical yet lavish with their praise, that they succeed in enthusing even the most jaded palate' – Arabella Boxer in *Vogue*

English Food - Jane Grigson

'Jane Grigson is perhaps the most serious and discriminating of her generation of cookery writers, and *English Food* is an anthology all who follow her recipes will want to buy for themselves as well as for friends who may wish to know about real English food … enticing from page to page' – Pamela Vandyke Price in the *Spectator*

Classic Cheese Cookery   Peter Graham

Delicious, mouth-watering soups, starters, main meals and desserts using cheeses from throughout Europe make this tempting cookery book a must for everyone with an interest in the subject. Clear, informative and comprehensive, it is a book to return to again and again.

READ MORE IN PENGUIN

GARDENING

The Well-Tempered Garden Christopher Lloyd

A thoroughly revised and updated edition of the great gardening classic. 'By far the best-informed, liveliest and most worthwhile gardener–writer of our time ... There is no reasonable excuse for any gardener failing to possess Christopher Lloyd's books' – *Interiors*

The Pip Book Keith Mossman

All you need is a pip and patience ... 'The perfect present for the young enthusiast, *The Pip Book* should ensure that even the most reluctant avocado puts down roots and sends up shoots' – *The Times*

The Good Plant Guide Brian Davis

When you are buying plants for your garden there are facts you need to know before selecting and purchasing. *The Good Plant Guide* provides information on almost every type of plant that you may want to purchase, including trees, shrubs, flowers, fruit and vegetables. No keen gardener can afford to be without this indispensable book.

Organic Gardening Lawrence D. Hills

The classic manual on growing fruit and vegetables without using artificial or harmful fertilizers. 'Enormous value ... enthusiastic writing and off-beat tips' – *Daily Mail*

READ MORE IN PENGUIN

GARDENING

The Adventurous Gardener Christopher Lloyd

Prejudiced, delightful and always stimulating, Christopher Lloyd's book is essential reading for everyone who loves gardening. 'Get it and enjoy it' – *Financial Times*

Gardens of a Golden Afternoon Jane Brown

'A Lutyens house with a Jekyll garden' was an Edwardian catch-phrase denoting excellence, something fabulous in both scale and detail. Together they created over 100 gardens, and in this magnificent book Jane Brown tells the story of their unusual and abundantly creative partnership.

A History of British Gardening Miles Hadfield

From the Tudor knot gardens through the formal realities of Jacobean and Georgian landscaping and on to the Gothic fantasies of wealthy Victorian landowners, Miles Hadfield brings the British gardens of the past vividly alive. 'An extraordinarily rich harvest of valuable and entertaining information ... it is hard to see that it can ever be superseded' – *Journal of the Royal Horticultural Society*

Plants from the Past David Stuart and James Sutherland

As soon as it is planted, even the most modern garden can be full of history, whether overflowing with flowers domesticated by the early civilizations of Mesopotamia or with plants collected in the Himalayas for Victorian millionaires. 'A thoroughly engaging style that sometimes allows bracingly sharp claws to merge from velvet paws'   – *World of Interiors*

READ MORE IN PENGUIN

A SELECTION OF HEALTH BOOKS

The Kind Food Guide Audrey Eyton

Audrey Eyton's all-time bestselling *The F-Plan Diet* turned the nation on to fibre-rich food. Now, as the tide turns against factory farming, she provides the guide destined to bring in a new era of eating.

Baby and Child Penelope Leach

A beautifully illustrated and comprehensive handbook on the first five years of life. 'It stands head and shoulders above anything else available at the moment' – Mary Kenny in the *Spectator*

Woman's Experience of Sex Sheila Kitzinger

Fully illustrated with photographs and line drawings, this book explores the riches of women's sexuality at every stage of life. 'A book which any mother could confidently pass on to her daughter – and her partner too' – *Sunday Times*

A Guide to Common Illnesses Dr Ruth Lever

The complete, up-to-date guide to common complaints and their treatment, from causes and symptoms to cures, explaining both orthodox and complementary approaches.

Living with Alzheimer's Disease and Similar Conditions
Dr Gordon Wilcock

This complete and compassionate self-help guide is designed for families and carers (professional or otherwise) faced with the 'living bereavement' of dementia.

Living with Stress
Cary L. Cooper, Rachel D. Cooper and Lynn H. Eaker

Stress leads to more stress, and the authors of this helpful book show why low levels of stress are desirable and how best we can achieve them in today's world. Looking at those most vulnerable, they demonstrate ways of breaking the vicious circle that can ruin lives.

READ MORE IN PENGUIN

A SELECTION OF HEALTH BOOKS

When a Woman's Body Says No to Sex Linda Valins

Vaginismus – an involuntary spasm of the vaginal muscles that prevents penetration – has been discussed so little that many women who suffer from it don't recognize their condition by its name. Linda Valins's practical and compassionate guide will liberate these women from their fears and sense of isolation and help them find the right form of therapy.

Medicine The Self-Help Guide
Professor Michael Orme and Dr Susanna Grahame-Jones

A new kind of home doctor – with an entirely new approach. With a unique emphasis on self-management, *Medicine* takes an active approach to drugs, showing how to maximize their benefits, speed up recovery and minimize dosages through self-help and non-drug alternatives.

Defeating Depression Tony Lake

Counselling, medication, and the support of friends can all provide invaluable help in relieving depression. But if we are to combat it once and for all, we must face up to perhaps painful truths about our past and take the first steps forward that can eventually transform our lives. This lucid and sensitive book shows us how.

Freedom and Choice in Childbirth Sheila Kitzinger

Undogmatic, honest and compassionate, Sheila Kitzinger's book raises searching questions about the kind of care offered to the pregnant woman – and will help her make decisions and communicate effectively about the kind of birth experience she desires.

Care of the Dying Richard Lamerton

It is never true that 'nothing more can be done' for the dying. This book shows us how to face death without pain, with humanity, with dignity and in peace.